Introduction to Coding in Hours With JavaScript

LEVEL 1

A Guide to Programming for Students With No Prior Experience

Written by:

Jack C. Stanley and Erik D. Gross,
Co-Founders of The Tech Academy

TABLE OF CONTENTS

TABLE OF CONTENTS

TABLE OF CONTENTS

TABLE OF CONTENTS

INTRODUCTION

Welcome to the first book in our series of introductory JavaScript texts!

We (Jack and Erik) took it upon ourselves to write this book in a way that is understandable to non-technical individuals and we wanted to create a resource for those who have never written code before. Many introductory programming books out there assume too much prior knowledge on the part of the reader. We instead attempted to write in a way that our non-tech savvy friends, family, and associates could comprehend and follow. As an example of this, one of our benchmarks in developing chapters and assignments was: "Could our parents do this?"

The two primary barriers to entry into the tech industry are:

1. The massive required technical vocabulary of over 1,000 terms (which some people spew out with no concern for their audience), and

2. The tendency of some experts to talk down to beginners or the "uninitiated" in a way that belittles their knowledge level and is over their heads. A sort of clique mentality can form with experienced programmers that acts as a buffer against new entries to the team.

So, this book stands as a rebellion against "business as usual" – we instead assume no prior technical knowledge on the part of the reader, and we will explain and define every technical term and concept in plain English.

It is notable that the logo of our school (The Tech Academy) contains a bridge. This bridge not only pays homage to the city we are headquartered in (Portland, Oregon – which is sometimes referred to as "Bridge City" or "Bridgetown"), it represents a passage of the gap between general society and technically-trained individuals. The Tech Academy bridge is a path that leads to an understanding of technology and competence in coding.

Instead of throwing you right into writing code, we are going to lay a foundation for you to build upon by breaking down fundamental terms and concepts that will open the door for an understanding of the actions you will take into this book. Or put another way, instead of turning you into a "coding parrot" who simply types what we tell them to, we are going to prepare you to actually comprehend what you are doing as you do. Therefore, you will not write any code until the second chapter of this book.

So, without further ado, let's dive in and start with the fundamentals, including what terms like *program* and *code* really mean.

CHAPTER 1
CODING TERMS

In order to write code, we need a *computer*. So, let's briefly discuss what a computer is. As you know, it is a machine (equipment with a purpose; a tool).

Computers were created to do a simple thing: they take in data (information), change the data in some way, and send out data. That's all.

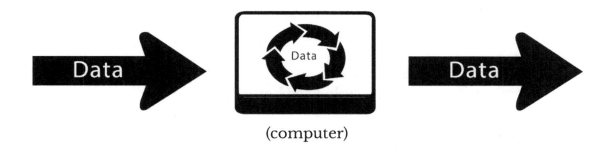

(computer)

As machines, some of the characteristics of computers include the following:

- They handle *data*. Again, data is information – such as words, symbols (something written that represents an amount, idea, or word), pictures, etc.

- They obey *instructions* (commands entered into them that perform certain tasks).

- They *automate* (perform actions without human interaction) tasks that would either take too long for a person to do or be too boring or repetitive.

- They *process* data. Process means to handle something through use of an established (and usually routine) set of procedures. When a computer displays the word "processing", it is simply saying, "Hold on while I perform some pre-established procedures." Processing refers to "taking actions with data." Searching through words to locate typos would be an example of processing data.

When computers perform actions, it is referred to as *executing* or *running*. For example, you can run a search on the internet by clicking the search button, or you could execute an instruction by pressing enter on your keyboard.

THE PURPOSE OF COMPUTERS IS TO TAKE IN DATA, PROCESS IT AND SEND IT OUT.

The point where computers really started to become valuable to people was when it was worked out how to install programs on them.

Install means to put something inside a computer that the computer can then use.

Programs are sets of written instructions, entered into a computer by people, that make it execute specific tasks. Installing a program means to put it into a computer so that the program can execute. For example, you could install a program by transferring the data that makes up the program from the internet to your computer.

Behind every action you perform on a computer, there is a program. Common programs you have probably used before include:

- Microsoft Word (a program that allows you to type documents)

- Google Chrome (a program that helps you search the internet)

- iTunes (a program used to organize and listen to music)

Programs are written in a *programming language*. A programming language is an organized system of words, phrases, and symbols that lets you create programs. Just as there are many languages used by people across the world, there are different types of programming languages. In fact, there are over a thousand programming languages (though only about ten account for the majority of languages used).

In the same way that hammers and ladders have specialized utilizations, each programming language has different uses. For example, some programming languages were designed mainly to improve websites, while others were made for creating computer games.

The instructions inside these programs are referred to as *code*. Most code originally looks similar to English and is then translated down to instructions composed of the 1s and 0s that computers understand (called *machine language*).

For example, to have a computer display the words "Hello!" on your screen using Python (a popular computer programming language used to create programs and websites), the code is written as:

```
print("Hello!")
```

When someone says "program a computer" or "do some coding," they are just saying, "Write a set of instructions into a computer, using a programming language, that will result in specific actions being performed when that set of instructions is called for."

A *computer programmer* is one who engages in computer programming (writing code that results in programs). Programmers are also referred to as *coders*, *software developers,* and *software engineers.*

Coders create *software*, which is just another word for "program" or "application". These terms are all interchangeable – though "app" (abbreviation of application) is usually used to refer to programs (applications; software) on a mobile device (like a cell phone).

Computer programs are saved as *files*. As you may already know, files are collections of data stored on a computer. Files each have their own name and contain their own data, and they often are collected together in a *folder*. Folders are used to organize files on a computer and are given their own name. Another word for folder is *directory*. For example, an application could consist of multiple files all saved in the same directory (folder).

WHAT IS JAVASCRIPT?

JavaScript is a widely-used programming language that works on most computers and is especially important for web development (creating and managing websites). It is primarily used to make websites interactive (allowing them to respond to user actions or other factors), rather than being static (unchanging; unmoving). For example, JavaScript can make a button change color when clicked, or can cause a video to start playing when a user hovers their mouse over it.

While its main use is to enhance websites, JavaScript is also employed in creating a variety of computer programs. Its flexibility and compatibility make it one of the most popular languages for web developers and computer programmers.

Here are some real-world use cases of JavaScript:

- Facebook: JavaScript powers the interactive design and real-time (live; with no delay) updates, like comments and notifications.

- Gmail: JavaScript handles actions like email loading and search, without reloading the page.

- YouTube: JavaScript controls elements such as video playback and recommendations on the site.

- PayPal: JavaScript helps manage payments and various interactive features on the website.

Let's briefly discuss the history of JavaScript. In the mid-1990s, there was no Google, and so, prior to Google Chrome, the most popular browser (software used to access and view websites) was Netscape Navigator. JavaScript was created by Brendan Eich in 1995, who worked for Netscape at the time. Originally, JavaScript was created as the programming language for Netscape in order to improve their browser and user experience (ease of usability of their software).

One of the inspirations for the name "JavaScript" at the time was the prominent programming language *Java* (which is used to create applications that can run on many different types of devices). To be clear: Java and JavaScript are two completely different languages, but in order to piggyback on the popularity of Java, Netscape named the new language JavaScript.

The *script* in JavaScript refers to the fact that JavaScript can be used to write scripts. *Scripts* are small programs that automate tasks or make websites interactive by responding to user actions. For example, a script could be written in JavaScript that updates the shopping cart total on a website when a user adds or removes items, without needing to reload the entire page.

There are numerous uses for JavaScript and (as was mentioned earlier) it is utilized in the creation of many different types of computer programs.

HTML AND CSS

JavaScript is one of three of the main technologies utilized to create content on the World Wide Web, with *HTML* and *CSS* being the other two. HTML creates the structure (layout; framework) of webpages, CSS handles the design (stylistic items, like fonts and colors), and JavaScript manages the functionality (operations; interactivity).

Since using JavaScript is usually utilized in conjunction with HTML/CSS, let's take a deeper dive into these tools.

HTML (Hypertext Markup Language) is the standard language used to create and structure content on web pages (text, images, links, etc). Let's break down the components of this term:

- *Hypertext* is the text on a webpage that links to other text or a resource (any external content, such as an image, video, document, or another webpage), allowing users to navigate between them. Hypertext links are typically styled as blue text with an underline.

  The "hyper" in "hypertext" means "beyond" or "more than," which refers to the fact that the text can include links to other texts, allowing for easy navigation between related content.

- *Markup language* is a system of symbols used to define the structure and content of a document, like a webpage. The term *markup* originates from the traditional publishing process, where editors would "mark up" a manuscript with symbols to indicate formatting instructions for printers. Markup is the special symbols (code) used to tell a computer how to display or format text and other content. Markup languages utilize *tags*.

  Tags are how the markup of the content in the HTML document is specified. The basic principle is this: If you put special instructions before and after the content you want to affect, another program can tell the difference between the instruction and the content, and can then present the data in a specified manner. Because of this, tags usually have two parts: an opening tag and a closing tag. The content goes in between these two tags. Opening tags indicate the beginning of a markup instruction and closing tags indicate the end.

  Opening tags are written as a "less than" angle bracket (<), followed by the markup instruction, and then a "greater than" angle bracket (>). An example would be the tag used to make text **bold**. The actual instruction is the word "strong," meaning "make the text controlled by this tag stand out," usually by making it bold. The opening "strong" tag would look like this: <**strong**>

  You also need to specify a closing tag, so the computer program knows when to stop bolding the text and that is where the closing tag comes in. Closing tags use the same instruction as the opening tag, but with a forward slash (/) placed before the instruction (</>). The closing "strong" tag would look like this: </**strong**>

Putting all the parts together, if you wanted to emphasize a quote, you would write the markup language code (in this example, we will use the markup language HTML) like this: "Education is the most powerful weapon which you can use to change the world."

The output (result; display) of this markup language (which again was HTML in this example) would be:

"Education is the most powerful weapon which you can use to change the world."
-Nelson Mandela

So, to summarize, a tag is a piece of code, usually enclosed in angle brackets (e.g., <tag>), that tells a web browser how to structure, display, or format content on a webpage. And, again, a markup language is a way to structure, format, and annotate (label; describe) text in a document using tags so that computers can display or process it correctly. HTML is a markup language that utilizes hyperlinks (clickable links that take you to another webpage).

Now that we have defined HTML, let's further explore its partner, CSS (Cascading Style Sheets), by dissecting its component parts in reverse order:

- A *style sheet* is a set of rules that tells a web page how to look (such as colors, fonts, and layout). The word *style* refers to the visual design, and *sheet* refers to a list or collection of these design rules, which is usually contained in a separate file from other code.

- The term *cascading* originates from the idea of a waterfall, where water flows down in levels or steps. In the context of CSS, cascading is used to describe how styles "flow down" in a sequence, where rules are applied one after another (similar to how water cascades over different levels) with later or more specific rules potentially overriding (replacing; dominating) earlier ones.

And so, CSS is a language used to define the visual appearance of a web page, where the cascading aspect allows multiple style rules to be applied in a prioritized order, and the style sheet is a collection of these design rules. CSS is used to control the appearance and layout of web pages, allowing you to style elements like colors, fonts, spacing, etc.

HTML, CSS, and JavaScript are used in combination with each other to create dynamic (changing or updating automatically while being used) websites.

Consider this image, which shows that HTML as the structure of the car, CSS as the appearance (e.g., color), and JavaScript as the function (engine):

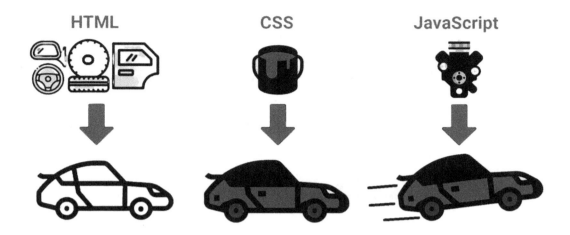

WHERE DO YOU WRITE YOUR CODE?

As you know, all software (applications; programs) are made up of code. As a user (the person using software), you do not see the code. So where is it, and how is it written? Well, the three most common types of programs that developers use to write their code in are:

1) **Integrated development environment (IDE):** A *development environment* is a set of tools and software that is used for coding, testing, and debugging applications effectively. *Integrated* refers to the fact that the tools are combined into a single location, where they work together seamlessly. And so, an *IDE* is a software application that combines tools to streamline and simplify the process of writing, testing, and managing code in one unified location. For example, Visual Studio (available from Microsoft) is a popular IDE:

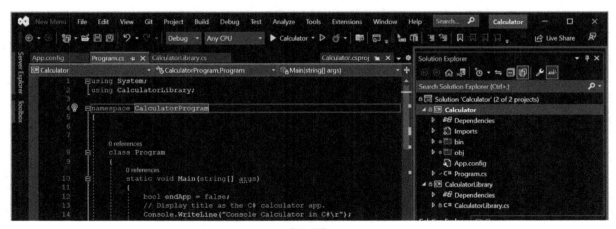

(IDE)

2) **Text editor:** A program used to write and edit text. Text editors are very basic – meaning, the text is typically plain with no effects. This is technically different from a word processor, which is a program on a computer that allows you to create, format (design the style and layout), modify, and print documents. While text editors can be used to write code, word processors cannot. Instead, word processors have more functionality (ability to perform a wider array of actions) than text editors. Below on the left you can see Microsoft Word (a word processor), while Notepad (on the right) is a text editor.

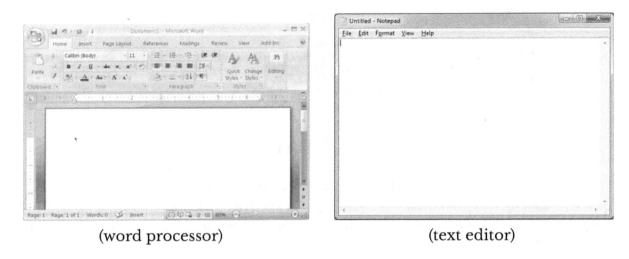

(word processor)   (text editor)

Out of the three programs included on this list that people can use to write code within, text editors are the least used and are not recommended.

3) **Code editor:** A program that can be used to write/edit code. Code editors are in between IDEs and text editors in terms of features (functions built into an application) – they have fewer features than an IDE but more than a text editor. One of the most popular code editors is Notepad++ (plus plus). As an example, the popular IDE Visual Studio has a feature called "LiveShare", which allows developers to share their code with others as it is being written. This feature is not included in the code editor Notepad++. On the other hand, Notepad++ has a useful feature called "auto-completion", which suggests various options for completing the code you are typing. For example, when you type *pr*, auto-completion may suggest *print*. This feature does not exist in the text editor Notepad.

(code editor)

Due to its ease of use and popularity, we will write our code using the code editor Notepad++ in this book.

<u>VALUE TYPES</u>

A *value* refers to the specific piece of data stored in a program (such as a number or text).

Value type (also referred to as *data type*) is a classification that specifies the kind of value a piece of data can hold (such as a number, text, or true/false statement) and how it can be used in programming.

Whereas a data type defines what kind of data you can use and the rules for how it behaves, a value is an actual example of that type. For example, *5* is a value which is part of the number data type.

Here are the main value types (data types) that are built into the JavaScript programming language:

- **Number:** A type of value used to represent any kind of number, including whole numbers and decimals. EXAMPLE: A person's age (such as **39**) is the *number* data type.

- **String:** A sequence of text characters (like words, sentences, or symbols) enclosed in quotation marks. EXAMPLE: **"Hello, world!"** is the *string* value type.

- **Boolean:** A value that can only be either *true* or *false*, used for making decisions in code. EXAMPLE: A true-or-false statement, like "Is it raining?" (where the accepted answers are either true or false) would be the *boolean* data type.

- **Undefined:** A placeholder (temporary label) for something that has been named but not yet given any content or value. EXAMPLE: If a program asks, "What is your name?" and no answer is given, that missing answer is an *undefined* value type.

- **Null:** A special value used to show that something is empty or has no value on purpose. EXAMPLE: If a search for a user in a database (organized collection of data) does not find any matching results, the program could return *null* to indicate that no user was found. As a note, *return* means to send a result or value back.

- **BigInt:** A type of number used for very large integers (whole numbers) that are too big for regular numbers. EXAMPLE: One trillion-trillion (which regular numbers cannot easily represent) would be a *BigInt* value type.

- **Symbol:** A special value that is always unique and is used to label or identify different (separate) pieces of data. EXAMPLE: In a program that manages a list of users, *symbols* (for example, user1, user2, user3, etc.) could be used as a unique identifier (special name; distinct label) for each user to ensure that no two users share the same identifier, even if they have the same name.

- **Object:** A collection of related data or information that can include numbers, text, lists, and even other things. EXAMPLE: A profile containing a person's name, age, and occupation is an *object* because it groups multiple pieces of related information.

These data types will make more sense as we write them out in actual code later in this book, but for now you have the basic definitions in place.

CHALLENGES

At the end of most chapters, we have included an "END OF CHAPTER CHALLENGE." These are opportunities for you to put together all that you studied in each chapter. At times, you will also be instructed to figure out solutions to problems on your own. Working software developers are often assigned projects and tasks they have never done before and so a key element of the job is researching solutions online.

Some of these challenges will have you repeat tasks you have already performed. The reasons for such repetition are to provide you with an opportunity to create your own approach, and allow you to better understand and remember code through additional practice.

CODING TIPS

We are nearing the end of this chapter and you will be writing code in no time! If you run into any trouble while going through this book, here are some tips:

1. Make sure your code is written *exactly* as it is in the book. The smallest error in your code (such as a missing comma or an extra symbol) can wreck the whole program. Code must be exact for programs to run properly, so always meticulously check your code for errors.

2. Research online for solutions.

3. Ensure you understand all the terms being used – define any words you do not understand. Misunderstood terms can prevent understanding and cause mistakes, so research for definitions when needed.

4. You can contact The Tech Academy through our website and ask for assistance here: learncodinganywhere.com

Now that we have prepared you for what to expect, and laid the basic foundation of coding terms and concepts, we can begin writing code!

CHAPTER 2
GETTING STARTED WITH JAVASCRIPT

It is time to get our hands dirty and write some code! As was mentioned earlier, we will do so inside the code editor Notepad++.

From now on, each chapter will have you perform actions on your computer – you will actually *do* things. We have written all assignments (things you are expected to do on your computer) **in bold in a different font.**

And so, here is your first task:

Download and install Notepad++ here: notepad-plus-plus.org

If you are using a Macintosh (Apple) computer, you can utilize a different code editor (such as Sublime Text or Brackets).

The first code that developers usually write when learning a new language is to make the computer display the text: "Hello, world." We are going to first use HTML to do this because (again) JavaScript is commonly used in conjunction with HTML (where HTML provides the structure, and JavaScript provides the functionality).

In HTML, the tags and the code written between them are called *elements*. Here is a diagram that showing this:

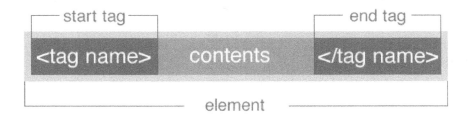

At the top of each HTML document containing HTML code is the <!DOCTYPE HTML> declaration. In HTML, a *declaration* is a statement that defines the type of document being used and provides important information for the browser.

The <!DOCTYPE HTML> declaration is not a tag (a special symbol used to define elements and structure) – it is an instruction to the browser telling it you are using HTML. There are other doctypes (types of documents) you could use, so clarifying that we are using HTML helps the browser out.

20

The <html> tag is inserted at the beginning of your code, and all your HTML code is contained in between it and the end tag (</html>).

The <body> tag denotes where you can add the contents of an HTML document (such as text, images, videos, lists, links, etc.).

Complete these steps:

1. Open Notepad++.

2. Click on File on the menu bar and open a New File (or just press Ctrl + N).

3. Inside Notepad++, write this code:

```
<!DOCTYPE HTML>
<html>
    <body>
    Hello, world!
    </body>
</html>
```

   (As a reminder, the "/" symbol in the code you wrote denotes an "end tag".)

4. Save this document by clicking on "File", then "Save As". Name the document Test.html and ensure you click on "Hypertext Markup Language" under "Save as type".

   (It is important to include .html at the end of all of your HTML code files because if you don't, your computer will not recognize that it is an HTML file and your code won't run. Also, make sure you save this file to your desktop.)

5. Run your code.

   There are various ways to run your code. One way is to right click on your file on the desktop and select "Open with" and navigate to Google Chrome.

You can also just drag and drop your HTML file into an open Google Chrome window, like this:

Note that the file icon (symbol above the file name) in the picture above is the Google Chrome logo, that is because on the computer the photo is taken from, Google Chrome is set as the default program used to open HTML files. The icon of your file may or may not be different.

From now on in this book, when we say *run* or *execute* your code, we mean to "Open it in Google Chrome" so you can see your webpage displayed in the browser.

For Mac users using Brackets, you can also click "File" and then "Live Preview" to run your code.

Congratulations! You made the browser display the text "Hello, world!"

PARAGRAPHS

In HTML, the <p> element is used to create paragraphs.

Complete these actions:

1. Open your HTML file and write this code within the body tag:

```
<body>
    <p>This is a paragraph!</p>
</body>
```

2. Save and execute your code.

Good job! You created a paragraph.

ONLINE IMAGES

A *Uniform Resource Locator (URL)* is a unique name for a web resource (an identifiable thing that can be found on the internet). The most common example of a URL is a website. For example, "https://www.google.com" is a URL.

An *attribute* is a word or phrase used inside an element's opening tag that controls the element's behavior. For example, the image <img> tag allows you to place images inside your webpage, and the src (source) attribute is used with this <img> tag to give the location of the image (where the image is being displayed from).

You can see the image tag and source attribute here:

```
<img src="https://www.petmd.com/sites/default/files/petmd-cat-happy-15.jpg">
```

In this code, the image tag tells the browser where to put the image on the page, while the src attribute gives the location to pull (use) the image from. You can pull images from online or from your computer. In the code above, we are grabbing it from the internet.

Perform these actions:

1. Find an image online that you would like to display in your HTML code and copy the image's URL.

   You can do this as follows:

   A. Search for the image you want on Google (such as "kitten").

   B. Click on "Images" under the search bar.

   C. Click on the image you want (it should then display on the right side of your screen).

   D. Right click on the image and select "Copy image address." Paste this URL somewhere because we will be using it soon.

2. Open up your Test.html file (if not already open, one way to do this is to right click on your file on the desktop and select Edit with Notepad++) and replace the code within the body tag with this image tag:

```
<body>
<img src = "insert the image's URL here"></img>
</body>
```

3. Save and execute your code. (Programmers always save their code before running it.)

Well done! Your image is displayed in the browser.

COMPUTER IMAGES

Characters are letters, numbers and symbols – such as those found on a keyboard.

The route to a file is written with characters, and such a route is called a *file path*. The file path is the address of a file and specifies the exact location of a file. It provides a "path" to the file.

File paths say things like, "You can find the file named 'Winter' inside the folder named 'Poems', which is inside the C drive." (A *drive* is simply a location where data is stored, and the *C drive* is where most files and software are stored on a computer.)

The various components of a path are separated by a text character that is not part of the name of a directory (folder) or a file. Usually this character is a slash (/), backslash (\ ) or colon (:).

The \ (backslash) symbol separates the different parts of a collection of electronic documents (files) in computers, and it was originally created as an aid to organizing and finding the various files you might store on a computer. In a file path, backslashes are used to show that one item is below another (in terms of hierarchy).

A *hierarchy* refers to arranging things according to rank or status. It refers to organizing items according to their relative importance or characteristics. *Storage hierarchy* refers to a system where various data storage devices are given a hierarchical importance ranking in terms of how they are used.

The primary factor influencing a given device's ranking is its response time (how long the device takes to return a requested piece of stored data when the computer requests the data). Faster response times are ranked "higher" and so are loaded/executed before others.

In a file path, the item on the left is "above" the one on the right. If we take our earlier example, the file path would be written as: **C:\Poems\Winter**

To prepare for the next assignment, download an image of your choosing (ensuring to save it in your Downloads folder) now.

Written documents, pictures, and videos are examples of different types of *file formats*. The data in these various file formats is organized in a specific way, usually based on how the data will be used by various processes the computer does. For example, the data in a file that is a written document will be organized in a very different way than the data in a file that is a video. A common file format is "PDF", which stands for "Portable Document Format". It is a file format developed by the software company Adobe in the 1990s to ensure consistent display of files regardless of what computer they are being displayed on.

File formats are indicated by their *extension*, which is code that states what the file format is (text, image, video, etc.). Extensions are tacked on at the end of the file's name. Let's say you have a file entitled "Contract" and it's stored as a PDF; the file would be named "Contract.pdf" (with .pdf being the extension). Another common file format and extension is ".txt" (short for "text file"). This is a file type that is pure, unformatted (no special design; plain) text. If you have ever used the application Notepad, it saves and runs .txt files.

As we covered earlier, your HTML files must always end with the .html extension.

If we want to display an image that is saved on your computer in our HTML code (as opposed to one stored online), we include the file path like this: **C:\Users\user\Downloads\File_Name.Extension**

To ensure you have the correct file path for your image, you can right-click the image and select "Properties" – you will see the file path to the image next to "Location:".

For example, if we saved a picture named "Kitten" in our Downloads folder, this could be the file path: **C:\Users\user\Downloads\Kitten.jpeg**

Jpeg is a type of image format and we must include the extension for the image in our file path – otherwise, the image will not display.

Complete these actions:

1. Open up your Test.html file and add this image tag between the body tags (ensure to include the custom file path to your image):

```
<body>
<img src = "C:\Users\user\Downloads\File_Name.Extension"></img>
</body>
```

2. Save and run your code.

   If it doesn't display correctly, check the following:

   A. Did you save your image in your Downloads folder? If not, move it there.

   B. Did you include the image file extension? If not, add it.

   C. Did you enter the correct file path? If not, verify it and add it.

Good job! You correctly displayed an image stored on your computer in the browser.

"HELLO, WORLD" IN JAVASCRIPT

How about we write some JavaScript now? Well, there are two ways we can add JavaScript to our HTML code. The first way is to just write the code inside the HTML using the <script> element.

The <script> tags mean we are inserting a script, and in between them is where we write our JavaScript code. As a reminder, a *script* is a set of instructions that automates tasks or controls the behavior of software or web pages.

In coding, an *object* is something that has state (condition; attribute) and behavior (action; procedure). For example, a "dog" object could have "awake" as its state and "barking" as its behavior.

A *method* is something an object can do – it is a named sequence of events.

A method should always have a meaningful name, such as *CalculateIncomeTax* (not *Method_1* or something else that's non-descriptive), that way you can get an idea of what the method is supposed to do from just reading the name.

alert() is a JavaScript method that displays an alert box (small window with an "OK" button). When using alert(), the *object* is the window (the box that will be displayed), whereas *alert* is the method (the action that displays the window).

As we mentioned earlier, *strings* (series of characters) are one of JavaScript's main value types. In JavaScript, we can create strings with double quotes (") or single quotes ('), such as: "Mary had a little lamb," or 'Its fleece was white as snow.' In the "Hello, world" code we wrote earlier, "Hello, world!" is a string. When writing code in JavaScript, it doesn't matter whether you use double or single quotes because they both perform the same functions.

Let's now use JavaScript within our HTML file to display "Hello, world"!

Complete these actions:

1. **Edit your HTML code file as follows (adding this script tag within the body tags):**

```
<script>
alert("Hello, World!");
</script>
```

2. **Save and execute this code.**

Good job! You just made a pop-up!

When we include our JavaScript code inside of our HTML file, it is called *inline* JavaScript because it is written "in line" with other code, as opposed to within a separate file.

<u>ANOTHER WAY</u>

An *alert window* is a small pop-up box in a web browser that displays a message to the user and requires them to acknowledge it before interacting with the page again. You created one in the preceding assignment.

We mentioned there are *two* ways to add JavaScript code to HTML. So let's now look at the second way: connecting our code to an external file. Meaning, we save our HTML code in its own HTML file, and our JavaScript code is located in a separate JavaScript file.

Complete these actions:

1. Create a new file and write this code:

```
alert("Hello, World!");
```

(This is our JavaScript code.)

2. Save this file on your desktop. Save it as "Test_1," as a "JavaScript file" (i.e., click File, Save As, write "Test_1" as the File name, and then click on JavaScript file under "Save as type"). The file should end with the .js extension (Test_1.js).

3. To link our HTML file to our JavaScript file, we use the `<script>` element with the src attribute. As a reminder, *src* is short for "source" – meaning, we are designating the source (location/name) of the file we are linking to. To do this, go back to your original HTML file and write this code within the body tags (edit the script tag to this):

```
<script src="Test_1.js">
</script>
```

4. Save and execute the HTML file. (We do *not* execute our .js file in the browser, we execute the .html file.)

Nicely done! We displayed the same alert window in a different way.

Keeping your JavaScript code in a separate file from your HTML code is the recommended way to organize your code and is considered the best practice.

So, as a recap, we can execute our JavaScript in two ways:

1) **Inline JavaScript** (all your JavaScript code contained within your HTML file), or

2) **External JavaScript** (JavaScript code kept in a separate file and referenced [referred to] in your HTML file). This keeps your HTML and JavaScript code in separate locations.

While the latter option is the way to go when doing professional software development, for simplicity's sake, we will use both of these methods throughout this book.

WINDOW.ALERT() METHOD

We can also cause an alert window to pop up using the window.alert() method.

In JavaScript, *statements* are the lists of instructions to be executed by the computer that make up a program. Statements are separated using a semicolon, which tells the computer, "Here is the end of this statement."

Complete these actions:

1. Edit the <script> element in your HTML file as follows:

```
<script>
window.alert("Hello, world!");
</script>
```

2. Save and execute your HTML file.

Excellent work!

DOCUMENT.WRITE() METHOD

We can display text in JavaScript using the document.write() method.

Complete these actions:

1. Edit the <script> element in your HTML file as follows:

```
<script>
document.write("Hello, world!");
</script>
```

2. Save and execute your code.

Very well done! As you can see, there is more than one way to perform actions in programming – problems can have multiple solutions.

END OF CHAPTER CHALLENGE

We have now reached the first challenge in this book. In this one, you are going to create some basic programs using the data covered in this chapter.

Perform these actions:

1. Create a webpage that has text and an image, and successfully run it in the browser.

2. Use an external JavaScript file (i.e., use <script src =""">) and document.write() to display text of your choosing.

CHAPTER 3
VARIABLES AND STRINGS

As a reminder, *value* refers to the specific piece of data stored in a program (such as a number or text).

A *variable* is a symbol or name that represents a value. In math, variables like "X" or "Y" are used to represent numbers in equations. Such as, "X + 2 = 5." (In this case, X is 3.)

In programming, variables store data values (such as numbers, text, or other types of information). They are called "variables" because their values can change (vary) as the program runs.

When coding, to *declare* a variable means to create it by giving it a name, so that it can store values later in the program.

Here is an example using pseudocode (words and symbols that look similar to code, but are just normal English – not actual code):

START
DECLARE variable 'age'
SET 'age' to 25
DISPLAY 'age'
SET 'age' to 30 (this changes the value from 25 to 30)
DISPLAY 'age'
END

This "program" declares a variable called age, sets its value to 25, displays 25, changes the value to 30, and then displays 30. Now consider this image, which shows variable names and values:

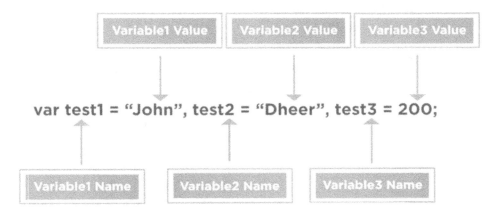

A common action in coding is to assign (declare) variables and they are key in every programming language.

In mathematics, an *operator* is a symbol used to carry out a computation (the act of figuring out the amount of something using math). There are several different kinds of operators, such as arithmetic operators like:

+ (add),

- (subtract),

/ (divide), and

* (multiply)

These arithmetic operators are used to perform math operations.

And, as a reminder, a *string* is a sequence of characters (such as letters, numbers, and symbols) used to represent text.

In JavaScript, the *assignment operator* is "=" and is used to assign value to a variable. For example, if we write X = 10 in JavaScript, we are assigning the variable "X" the value "10".

Let's assign a variable in JavaScript by performing these actions:

1. Update the <script> element within the HTML file as follows:

```
<script>
var X = "Hello, world!";
document.write(X);
</script>
```

2. Save and execute this code.

Way to go! We assigned the variable X= to the string value "Hello, world!"

CREATE A STRING

There are some characters that cannot easily be put within quotes when writing strings in JavaScript.

For example, what if you wanted to display: Sally said, "I don't want to go"? You not only have additional quotation marks around Sally's statement, but you also have the single quote (apostrophe) within "don't."

The solution to this problem is to add a backslash (\) – this is referred to as "escaping" the character and tells the computer that the character that follows has a special meaning. For example: \' or \" means that the quote mark(s) following the backslash will not end the string, but instead will be printed on the screen. So, again, to display single quote marks or double quotation marks in JavaScript, we use a backslash directly before them.

If you want to start a new line, you can use the HTML <br> tab, which is like pressing Enter.
 means *line break*. A line break literally creates a new line of text – again, like pressing Return/Enter on your keyboard.

Let's apply this data:

1. Update the <script> element within your HTML code file to this:

```
<script>
document.write("Lisa told Bart, \"Stop it, Bart! Or I'll tell dad!\"<br>\"Eat my shorts!\" Bart responded.");
</script>
```

2. Save and execute your code.

Good work! We have successfully displayed quotation marks and an apostrophe.

Now, what do you do if you need to display a backslash in your code? Simple, write two of them!: \\

CONCATENATING A STRING

Concatenate means to connect items together, like links in a chain. In programming, it means to take one piece of data and stick it on the end of another piece of data. For example, concatenating the string "dev" and the string "ices" makes the text "devices."

To concatenate a string in JavaScript, you use the + operator.

Complete these actions:

1. Update the <script> element within your HTML code file to the following:

```
<script>
document.write("\"Be who you are and say what you feel,"
+ "because those who mind don\'t matter and those who matter don\'t mind.\""
+ "-Dr. Seuss");
</script>
```

2. Save and execute your code. Something is not quite right… We are missing a space between "feel," and "because."

3. To fix this, simply add a space before "because" as follows:

```
" because those who mind don\'t matter and those who matter don\'t mind.\""
```

4. Save and execute your code again.

Great! Now it displays correctly.

MULTIPLE VARIABLES

You can also assign multiple variables in one statement.

Complete these actions:

1. Update the <script> element in your HTML file like this:

```
<script>
    var Family = "The Arezzinis", Dad = "Jeremiah",
        Mom = "Hermoine", Daughter = "Penny", Son = "Zorro";
    document.write(Dad);
</script>
```

2. Save and run your code.

Fantastic job! In this assignment, we assigned multiple variables and then displayed one.

FONT COLORS

We can change the font color of a string using the str.fontcolor method.

Complete these actions:

1. **Update the code in your HTML file as follows:**

```
<script>
    var blues = "I have the blues.";
    var blues = blues.fontcolor("blue");
    document.write(blues);
</script>
```

2. **Save and execute your code.**

Well done! We created a variable that was a string called "blues." We assigned that variable the color blue and then displayed it. See how that works?

END OF CHAPTER CHALLENGE

Write a program that does the following:

1. **Assigns multiple variables and displays one utilizing the document.write() method, and**

2. **Creates a string, concatenates a string and changes the string's font color.**

CHAPTER 4
EXPRESSIONS AND STATEMENTS

Expressions are numbers, symbols, and operators grouped together that show the amount of something. And as you likely know already, an *equation* is a mathematical statement that shows two expressions are equal, typically connected by an equals sign (=).

For example, **7 X 7** is an expression, and **7 X 7 = 49** is an equation.

In programming, an expression is a combination of values that are computed by the computer. Expressions can consist of variables, operators, and functions (blocks of code designed to perform specific tasks when run), and they return a value after being evaluated.

For example, **Name = "Data that the user types within the name box"** could be an expression. Also, **x + 5** is an expression.

As a reminder, *statements* are computer instructions. The simplest of these might be things like "print", "delete", "add", "multiply", etc. For example, the "print" statement tells your computer to print (display) whatever text you typed as part of the command.

In JavaScript, expressions and statements are different things. An expression results in a value, while a statement performs a task – a program is basically a series of statements.

There are two main types of expressions:

1) Ones that have a value (or result in a value), and

2) Those that assign a value to a variable.

This JavaScript code is an expression: **3 + 3**

Now, consider the following: **Document.write(3 + 3);**

This is a statement, and (within the statement) the expression 3 + 3 is contained.

Let's write a statement by completing these actions:

1. **Open your HTML file, and edit your `<script>` element like this:**

```
<script>
document.write(1 + 1);
</script>
```

2. **Save and execute your code.**

Wonderful! You just performed math with JavaScript and displayed the result.

FUNCTIONS

A *function* is a repeatable block of code that executes certain actions and performs tasks. You execute a function by calling it.

Call refers to executing a function or method so that it performs its defined task. This is also called *invoking* the function. *Invoke* literally means to request or ask for something. In coding, invoking (or calling) is to cause something to be carried out (performed).

In JavaScript, a *keyword* identifies actions to be performed. For example, there is a function keyword that is used to create functions.

Every spoken language has a general set of rules for how words and sentences should be structured. These rules are known as the *syntax* of that particular language. In programming languages, syntax serves the same purpose. Syntax is the rules you must follow when writing code. As you know, there are many languages you can use to program a computer, and each language has its own syntax. Failing to use the syntax of a particular language correctly can mean that whatever you are designing will not work at all.

The syntax for writing a JavaScript function is: the keyword, then the name, then parentheses.

Here is a diagram showing the proper syntax to create a function:

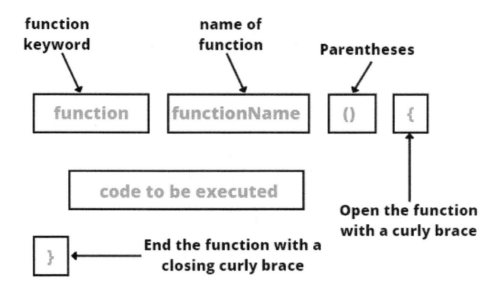

Functions are valuable because of code reusability – you can invoke functions over and over. Since functions in JavaScript contain properties (state) and methods (behavior), they are basically objects.

We will write a function shortly, but first let's define some additional, relevant terms.

In HTML, the <h1>-<h6> elements create headings (section heads). <h1> is the largest font size and gets smaller with each higher number (<h2>, <h3>, etc.)

<h1> THIS IS AN H1 HEADING </h1>

<h2> THIS IS AN H2 HEADING </h2>

<h3> THIS IS AN H3 HEADING </h3>

<h4> THIS IS AN H4 HEADING </h4>

(etc.)

"Id" is short for "identification." The *id attribute* specifies a unique name for an HTML element.

For example, you can assign a specific <p> element the id (name) "paragraph" as follows:

```
<p id="paragraph">This is some text.</p>
```

Now that you have that id, you can reference (bring up; refer to) it in your code later. You will learn exactly how to do this, and why doing so is useful, shortly.

Ids are specific and you can only utilize one id per element. For example, you cannot assign the same <h1> element two different ids.

For example, this code would be incorrect because the same name is being used for each id:

```
<h2 id="heading"></h2>
<h3 id="heading"></h3>
```

Ids must be specific to one element and cannot contain any spaces.

The *document.getElementById method* returns an element. It is a method that retrieves an HTML element by its unique id attribute, allowing you to access and use that specific element throughout your code. The element has an id attribute with a specific value assigned to it. It is used mainly to control or get information from an element within your code. If a document.getElementById method cannot find the element with the specified value, it will return "null." Null means "having a value of zero; no value."

You will understand it better once we put it into action soon.

To create a button, we can utilize the <button> element, which results in this:

Button

Now let's create a function and use the document.getElementById method.

Complete these actions:

1. **Open up your HTML code file, and edit the code within the `<body>` element like this:**

```
<body>
    <button onclick="My_First_Function()">
        Click me!
    </button>
    <p id="Irish"></p>
<script>
    function My_First_Function() {
        var String = "Kiss me, I'm Irish!";
        var result = String.fontcolor("green");
        document.getElementById("Irish").innerHTML =
        result;
    }
</script>
</body>
```

2. **Save and execute your code.**

Good work! You created a function and an operational button!

Take a moment to read through your code and try to figure out what we just did. Everything inside the curly brackets { } is our function. We used the ID attribute and assigned the button element the value "Irish." Then we returned the button element by calling the "Irish" value that we assigned earlier (when writing the ID attribute).

+= OPERATOR

The += operator can be used to concatenate a string like this:

1. **Edit the code within the `<body>` element as follows:**

```
<body>
    <p id="Concatenate"></p>
    <script>
    Sentence = "I am learning ";
    Sentence += "a lot from this course!";
    document.getElementById("Concatenate").innerHTML = Sentence;
    </script>
</body>
```

2. Save and execute your code.

Well done! You concatenated a string using the += operator.

END OF CHAPTER CHALLENGE

Complete these actions:

1. Write your own statement and ensure it displays a result.

2. Create a program that includes the following:

    a. A function, and

    b. The document.getElementById() method.

CHAPTER 5
NUMBERS

For the sake of simplicity, we are going to keep our HTML and JavaScript files separate for the next few assignments.

Complete these actions:

1. Open your HTML file in Notepad++ (Test.html) and edit the code as follows:

```
<!DOCTYPE HTML>
<html>
    <body>
        <p id="Math"></p>
        <script src="Test_1.js">
        </script>
    </body>
</html>
```

2. Save the file.

From now on, we will refer to this file as your "HTML code" or "HTML file".

Binary is a form of counting and performing math that uses only two numbers. The word comes from the Latin word *binarius*, meaning "two together" or a "pair." All quantities in binary are represented by numbers that use a 1 and/or a 0. In fact, any number can be written in binary.

You can see this below:

Binary Number	Amount	Binary Number	Amount
0000	Zero	0110	Six
0001	One	0111	Seven
0010	Two	1000	Eight
0011	Three	1001	Nine
0100	Four	1010	Ten
0101	Five	1011	Eleven

The ones and zeros in a computer are called *bits*, which is short for "binary digits".

Bits are stored in computers using very small devices, each of which can change to represent either a 1 or a 0 (1 means a small device is on, and 0 means it is off).

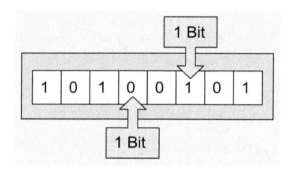

As we discussed earlier, one of the built-in JavaScript value types is "numbers". To store numbers, JavaScript uses 64 bits, which allows for 18,000,000,000,000,000,000 different numbers.

Arithmetic is the most common use of numbers in JavaScript. We already defined "operator", but as a reminder, an operator is a symbol used to carry out a computation. As was mentioned earlier, arithmetic operators include +, -, /, and *, and we can use these to perform math operations.

Let's put this into action by completing the following:

1. Open up your JavaScript file (Test_1.js – referred to as your "JavaScript code" for the next few steps) and write this code:

```
var Simple_Math = 2 + 2;
document.getElementById("Math").innerHTML = "2 + 2 = " + Simple_Math;
```

2. Save your code. As a reminder, if you run your JavaScript file, it won't work because you need to run your HTML file (which is linked to the JavaScript code).

3. Execute your HTML file.

Well done on performing math with JavaScript! Let's do some more.

SUBTRACTION

Now let's do some subtraction by performing these actions:

1. Edit your JavaScript code as follows:

```
var Simple_Math = 5 - 2;
document.getElementById("Math").innerHTML = "5 - 2 = " + Simple_Math;
```

2. Save your JavaScript code and execute the HTML file.

Good job on subtracting numbers with JavaScript!

MULTIPLICATION

Multiply numbers by doing the following:

1. Edit your JavaScript code as follows:

```
var Simple_Math = 6 * 8;
document.getElementById("Math").innerHTML = "6 X 8 = " + Simple_Math;
```

2. Save your JavaScript code and execute the HTML file.

Excellent work on performing multiplication with JavaScript!

DIVISION

And we can divide numbers as well. Complete these actions:

1. Edit your JavaScript code as follows:

```
var Simple_Math = 48 / 6;
document.getElementById("Math").innerHTML = "48 / 6 = " + Simple_Math;
```

2. Save your JavaScript code and execute the HTML file.

Voilà! Successful division. Now, what if you want to divide numbers that will have a remainder? (As a refresher, in division, the *remainder* is the amount left over after dividing two numbers. For example: 5 ÷ 2 would have a remainder of 1.)

The *modulus operation* finds the remainder after dividing two numbers.

As a reminder, a *dividend* is "the number being divided," and a *divisor* is "the amount the number is divided by." In our earlier example, 5 is the dividend and 2 is the divisor.

The term "modulus" comes from the Latin word *modulus*, meaning "measure." The modulus is the remainder after the dividend has been divided by the divisor. For example, in the expression 17 ÷ 5, the modulus is 2 because when 17 is divided by 5, the remainder is 2.

In JavaScript, the % symbol represents the modulus operator (which could also be called the remainder operator).

Let's put this to use by completing these actions:

1. Open up your JavaScript code and write the following:

```
var Simple_Math = 25 % 6;
document.getElementById("Math").innerHTML = "When you divide 25 by 6 you have a remainder of: "
    + Simple_Math;
```

2. Save your JavaScript code and execute the HTML file.

Nice work! You successfully performed division, with a remainder, using JavaScript.

MULTIPLE ARITHMETIC OPERATORS

Let's say you would like to multiply, subtract, add, *and* divide numbers all at once. Well, you can do so like this:

1. Edit your JavaScript code as follows (this is *one* way to do it):

```
var Simple_Math = (1 + 2) * 10 / 2 - 5;
document.getElementById("Math").innerHTML = "1 plus 2, multiplied by 10, " +
    "divided in half and then subtracted by 5 equals " + Simple_Math;
```

2. Save your JavaScript code and execute the HTML file.

Terrific job!

You included multiple operators in one block of code.

UNARY AND BINARY OPERATORS

Unary means "having, made up of, or acting on one component, item, or element."

An *operand* is the number that is being dealt with in a mathematical operation. It is not the action being taken with the number – it is the number itself. For example, in 5 + 6, the operands are 5 and 6, while "+" is the operator.

A *unary operator* is an operation that only contains a single operand. An example of this would be + 5.

A *binary operator* is an operation that requires two operands (one operand before the operator and one after). An example of this would be 5 + 5.

There is a unary operator called a *negation operator*. *Negate* literally means "to deny or contradict something." The word *negation* in "negation operator" means "negative; not positive." This returns the opposite or negative form of something. For example, in programming, applying the negation operator !true results in false, because the negation operator returns the opposite value. For instance, using the negation operator - on the number 5 returns -5 (which is the opposite or negative form of the positive number 5).

Let's write this code out in a new text document. Complete these actions:

1. Create a new HTML file and write this code:

```
<!DOCTYPE html>
<html>
    <body>
        <p id="Negation"></p>
        <script>
        var x = 10;
        document.getElementById("Negation").innerHTML = -x;
        </script>
    </body>
</html>
```

   (Note: the syntax for the negation operator is "-x".)

2. Save and execute your code.

There you go! You correctly used a negation operator.

INCREMENT AND DECREMENT

An *increment* is an addition or increase to something. "To increment" means to increase.

The *increment operator* in JavaScript is written as ++ and counts one step up.

The opposite of this is the *decrement operator*. *Decrement* basically means to count down.

Complete these actions:

1. In the HTML file you created in the preceding assignment, edit the <script> element as follows:

```
<script>
var X = 5;
X++;
document.write(X);
</script>
```

2. Save and execute your code.

Well done! It incremented from 5 to 6.

Now let's use the decrement operator by performing these actions:

1. In your HTML file, update the <script> element like this:

```
<script>
var X = 5.25;
X--;
document.write(X);
</script>
```

2. Save and run your code.

This results in "4.25." Good work!

MATH.RANDOM()

We can use JavaScript to generate a random number with the *Math.random()* method.

Complete these actions:

1. **To return a random number between 0 and 1, edit the <script> element within your HTML file as follows:**

```
<script>
window.alert(Math.random());
</script>
```

2. **Save and run your code.**

Good job! Now do this:

1. **To have a random number displayed between ____ and ____ (such as between 0 and 100), update the <script> element again like this:**

```
<script>
window.alert(Math.random() * 100);
</script>
```

2. **Save and run your code.**

Excellent! You used JavaScript to generate random numbers.

UNIQUE VALUES

In preparation for this coding assignment, let's complete a quick refresher about some math terms. *Factors* are numbers that can multiply together to get another number. For example, 4 and 5 are factors of 20 because 4 × 5 = 20.

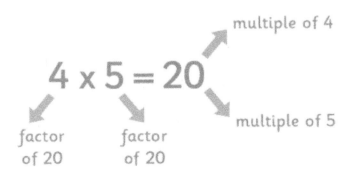

Superscripts are smaller characters, typically displayed toward the upper right of another number like this: **41^2**

Superscripts usually indicate "power." Power refers to how many times a number is multiplied by itself. For example, 10^4 means 10 to the fourth power – which is 10,000 (10 multiplied by 10 multiplied by 10 multiplied by 10).

A *notation* is a symbol or symbols used to represent numbers or amounts – such as an *E* placed at the end of a number. This notation means "10 to a given exponent." An *exponent* is the power to which a number is multiplied. In the 10^4 example given above, 4 is the exponent.

Here is a picture showing exponent and power (the total is 125):

A *floating point* is a specific way of representing large numbers. Instead of writing out the entire number, you can write the first part of it and then a factor to multiply it by. This makes it so that by performing the multiplication, you get essentially the same number you would have by writing it out in full. When you do this, you move the decimal point in the number; hence the name "floating point."

For example, take the number three thousand, four hundred twenty-five. Written normally, it would be: 3425. Written in floating point notation, it could be: 3.425×10^3. Since 10^3 is 1000, this means "3.425 times 1000" or 3425.

A *float* is a type of data used by computers that is used to store numbers with a very high degree of accuracy. It is primarily used for mathematical purposes.

Let's say we want a shorter way to write 10,000. We could write 10E 4.

10E 4 means 10 X 10^4 (10 multiplied by 10 four times). (As a reminder, *E* stands for exponent, which is how many times a number is multiplied by itself.)

In JavaScript, all numbers are floating point numbers, and the limit of floating point numbers is 1.797693134862315E+308 (meaning that JavaScript can not handle a larger floating point number). Any number that is larger than 1.797693134862315E+308 is considered "infinity."

As a note, 1.797693134862315E+308 is a massive number far beyond the capability of most calculators. It is about 179.77 quindecillion (a 1 followed by 308 zeros).

In JavaScript, there are three unique values that are considered to be numbers but they behave differently from regular numeric values:

1) NaN (short for "Not a Number")

2) Infinity (positive infinity)

3) -Infinity (negative infinity)

The best way to understand these is to put them into action, so go ahead and do the following:

1. Within the <body> element of an HTML file, write this code:

```
<body>
    <p id="Not_a_Number"></p>
    <script>
        document.getElementById("Not_a_Number").innerHTML = 0/0;
    </script>
</body>
```

2. Save your code and execute the file.

Perfect! The result is NaN because you can't divide 0 by 0.

We can check whether or not something is a number by using the isNaN() function, by doing this:

1. Now edit the code within the <body> element like this:

```
<body>
    <p id="Not_a_Number"></p>
    <script>
    document.getElementById("Not_a_Number").innerHTML = isNaN('Hello World');
    </script>
</body>
```

2. Save and run your code.

Precisely! As you can see, the result is "true" because "Hello World" is *not* a number.

Next, do these actions:

1. Change the code within your <body> element to the following:

```
<body>
    <p id="Not_a_Number"></p>
    <script>
    document.getElementById("Not_a_Number").innerHTML = isNaN('007');
    </script>
</body>
```

(Note: the only difference was that we changed "Hello World" to "007.")

2. Save and run your code.

Now it is false because 007 *is* a number.

INFINITY

Let's display "infinity" by completing these actions:

1. Update the code within the <body> element of your HTML file to this:

```
<body>
    <p id="Infinity"></p>
    <script>
    document.getElementById("Infinity").innerHTML = 1.7976931348623157E+309;
    </script>
</body>
```

2. Save and execute your code.

Good! You can see the result "infinity." This is because we entered a number larger than 1.797693134862315E+308.

To display "negative infinity" (-Infinity), simply change your code to a number lower than -1.797693134862315E+308.

Here is an example of code that would return -Infinity:

```
<body>
    <p id="Infinity"></p>
    <script>
    document.getElementById("Infinity").innerHTML = -1.7976931348623157E+309;
    </script>
</body>
```

END OF CHAPTER CHALLENGE

Complete these actions:

1. Write a program that includes the following:

   a. A binary operator,

   b. A unary operator,

   c. The modulus operator,

   d. Math.random(), and

   e. The increment or decrement operator.

   NOTE: Ensure that each of the above displays (prints) the result.

2. Create your own program that returns the following:

   a. Infinity,

   b. -Infinity, and

   c. NaN.

CHAPTER 6
DICTIONARIES

We talked about objects earlier – items that can be represented in a computer program and are often meant to represent real-world things.

You are surrounded by objects (your dog, the TV, etc.), and objects have *state* and *behavior*. The state of an object would be its characteristics – its attributes. The behavior of an object would be what the object does – the actions it takes.

A race car could be an object. Its state could be items like: engine type, engine horsepower, wheel size, gas tank capacity, etc. While its behavior could include: accelerate, decelerate, turn right, turn left, etc.

Let's look at a further example: an application might work with a "Customer" object. It could have states like "active" or "deleted." It could have behavior like "Upgrade Rewards Level" or "Add to Family Account."

Objects are one of the first subjects programmers think about when designing a program.

An object is something on a computer that you can click on, interact with, move around, etc. It can also be something behind the scenes that is made up of data and procedures to manipulate data. An object is what actually runs in the computer.

As another example, let's say you wanted to make two different types of cars on a computer; each car would be an object. Each object (car) would have its own size, shape, color, speed, distance it could travel without needing more gas, etc.

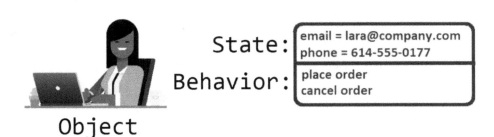

In JavaScript, a *dictionary* is a specialized type of list. A dictionary is essentially an object.

In a dictionary, the first item is the *key* (a unique identifier for some item of data), and the second item is the *value* (the data that is identified by the key). Together, they are a *key-value pair*.

"Key-value pair" is abbreviated "KVP." A KVP is a set of two linked data items that (again) consists of: a key and the value. Again, the key is the unique name, and the value is its content.

Collections of KVPs (i.e., dictionaries) are often used in computer programs.

Below is an example of a collection of KVPs that might be used in a computer program for a school. Here, the KEY is used to store the name of a course at the school, and the VALUE is the description of the course – this is a dictionary:

KEY	VALUE
INTRO_TO_PHYSICS	Basic physics principles.
WORLD_HISTORY	Global historical events.
ALGEBRA_I	Equations and graphing.
ENGLISH_LITERATURE	Study of literary works.
BIOLOGY	Cells and ecosystems.

Note that in this dictionary, you could not have a second Key-Value Pair that used the "BIOLOGY" key or "WORLD_HISTORY" key because each key in a given collection of KVPs must be unique.

And so, a "dictionary" is "a key-value pair collection."

In a dictionary, multiple values can be assigned to one key. This can be useful because you can look up various values by their key. In the below example, each key has three values assigned to it:

KEY	VALUES
0	Eddard Stark | 35 years old | Male
1	Cersei Lannister | 32 years old | Female

| 2 | Jon Snow \| 18 years old \| Male |
| 3 | Daenerys Targaryen \| 20 years old \| Female |

Let's put this into action by performing these actions:

1. **Open up Test.html. To create a dictionary in JavaScript, write this code within the <body> element:**

```
<body>
    <p id="Display"></p>
    <script>
    var Animal = {
        Species: "Dog",
        Color: "Black",
        Breed: "Labrador",
        Age: 5,
        Sound: "Bark!"
    };
    document.getElementById("Display").innerHTML = Animal.Sound;
    </script>
</body>
```

(NOTE: Due to the fact that 5 is the value type "number", not a string, we don't have to place it within quotation marks.)

2. **Save and execute your code.**

The output is: Bark! because this was associated with the key "Sound."

OPERATORS AS WORDS

As a reminder, an *operator* is a symbol or keyword (word that has a specific purpose and cannot be used as a variable name) used to perform an action or operation on one or more values, such as addition, comparison, or logical evaluation (true or false), etc.

Most operators are written as symbols: +, -, /, etc., but some are words. An example of this is the *delete* operator.

The delete operator in JavaScript is used to remove a property from an object.

58

Complete these actions:

1. Edit your previous code to the following:

```
<body>
    <p id="Delete"></p>
    <script>
        var Animal = {
            Species: "Dog",
            Color: "Black",
            Breed: "Labrador",
            Age: 5,
            Sound: "Bark!"
        };
        delete Animal.Sound;
        document.getElementById("Delete").innerHTML = Animal.Sound;
    </script>
</body>
```

2. Save and execute your code.

Good job! We deleted the value associated with the key Animal, so "undefined" is returned because the value is no longer defined in our dictionary, which is exactly what we wanted to accomplish.

ASSIGNING MULTIPLE VALUES

As was covered in the earlier description of dictionaries, we can assign multiple values to our keys. Complete these actions:

1. Edit the code within the <body> element to the following:

```
<body>
    <p id="Display"></p>
    <script>
    var Food = {
        Vegetables:["broccoli", " carrot", " lettuce"],
        Meat:["hotdog", " steak", " hamburger"],
        Fruit:["strawberry", " orange", " apple"],
        Quantity:[10, 21, 182],
    };
    document.getElementById("Display").innerHTML = Food.Fruit;
    </script>
```

2. Save and execute your code.

Excellent work on assigning more than one value to each of the keys in your dictionary!

TYPE OF OPERATOR

The *typeof operator* gives the value type of a variable. As a reminder, value type refers to the kind of data a variable can hold (such as a number, string, undefined, etc.).

Complete these actions:

1. **Edit the code with the <body> element as follows:**

```
<body>
    <script>
    document.write(typeof "This is a string");
    </script>
</body>
```

2. **Save and execute your code.**

3. **Now change your typeof operator to this:**

```
document.write(typeof 247365);
```

4. **Save and execute your code again.**

Excellent work! We successfully displayed the data types used.

END OF CHAPTER CHALLENGE

Complete these actions:

1. **Write a program that includes a dictionary.**

2. **Delete a KVP from your dictionary using the delete operator.**

3. **Use the typeof operator.**

4. **Try to create a dictionary with two identical keys, then attempt to display the keys using the document.getElementById() method and see what happens.**

CHAPTER 7
COMPARISONS

As you know, *logic* refers to actions, behavior, and thinking that makes sense. When speaking about computers, logic is the rules that form the foundation for a computer in performing certain tasks. Computer logic is the guidelines the computer uses when making decisions.

Logical operators like "and", "or", and "not" are used to evaluate whether an expression is true or false.

George Boole was an English mathematician that developed *Boolean logic*. Boolean logic is a form of logic in which the only possible results of a decision are "true" and "false." There are not any vague or "almost" answers to a calculation or decision – black or white, no gray. An example of Boolean logic would be answering questions with only "yes" or "no."

(George Boole)

Boolean logic is especially important for the construction and operation of digital computers because it is relatively easy to create a machine where the result of an operation is either "true" or "false." This is done by comparing two or more items – items that can only be "true" or "false."

Some common examples of such Boolean comparisons are "AND" and "OR". With the Boolean comparison called "AND", the comparison is true only if *all* of the involved comparisons are true.

Let's look at some examples to show how this works.

In the following AND comparison, the result is true: **5 is more than 3 AND 10 is more than 5**.

Let's break this down. There are three comparisons happening here:

1) Comparing 5 and 3 to see if 5 is larger than 3 (is 5 larger than 3?)

2) Comparing 10 and 5 to see if 10 is larger than 5 (is 10 larger than 5?)

3) Comparing the results of those two comparisons, using the Boolean comparison "AND" (are both comparisons true?). This is the overall comparison.

It is true that 5 is greater than 3, so the first comparison is true. It is also true that 10 is greater than 5 – so the second comparison is true as well.

A Boolean AND comparison is true if the other comparisons are all true – so in this example, the overall comparison is true, since the first comparison is true and the second comparison is also true.

In this next example, the result is false (not true): **5 is more than 7 AND 10 is more than 5**.

Even though 10 is more than 5, 5 is not more than 7 – so the overall comparison is not true.

A *condition* is an item that must be true before something else occurs. In the AND comparison above, these are the two conditions checked for:

1) 5 is more than 7

2) 10 is more than 5

They are conditions because the outcome is conditional upon (dependent on) these two comparisons.

A Boolean OR comparison checks for whether one or both conditions are true. Here is an example: **4 is less than 9 OR 8 is less than 7**.

The result would be true because at least one of the comparisons is true (4 is a smaller number than 9).

In the following example, the result would be false since neither is true: **8 is less than 4 OR 9 is less than 3.**

And in this example, the result would be true because one or both (in this case both) are true: **7 is less than 8 OR 2 is less than 5.**

As a reminder, in writing instructions for a computer, we would use the greater and lesser symbols (> and < respectively). For example: 7 > 3 means "seven is greater than three," and 4 < 9 means "four is less than nine."

So, for example, instead of 10 is greater than 2, we would write: **10 > 2**

If we wanted to say "greater than or equal to," we could use this symbol: >=

For example: **10 >= 8**

This would be true.

Here is a diagram showing Boolean logic applied to search terms:

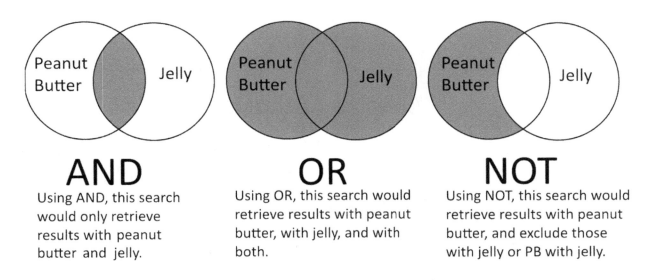

AND	OR	NOT
Using AND, this search would only retrieve results with peanut butter and jelly.	Using OR, this search would retrieve results with peanut butter, with jelly, and with both.	Using NOT, this search would retrieve results with peanut butter, and exclude those with jelly or PB with jelly.

TRUE AND FALSE

Like virtually all other programming languages, the Boolean values in JavaScript are true and false.

Let's put it into action by doing the following:

1. Open up an HTML file and edit the code within the <body> element to this:

```
<body>
    <script>
    document.write(10 > 5);
    </script>
</body>
```

2. Save and execute this code.

Great! You should see "true" displayed. That is because it is true that 10 is larger than 5.

If we change our code to the following, we will see "false":

```
<body>
    <script>
    document.write(10 < 5);
    </script>
</body>
```

This is Boolean logic!

CONSOLE.LOG METHOD

The console.log method can be used to display data in the console within the browser. The console is a tool you can use within your browser to debug code.

You can access the console in a few ways, including:

1) Pressing the F12 key and then clicking on "Console," or

2) Clicking the three upright dots in the top-right of the browser, selecting "More tools," clicking "Developer tools," and then selecting "Console."

Perform these actions:

1. Update the code within your <body> element as follows:

```
<body>
    <script>
    console.log(2 + 2);
    </script>
</body>
```

2. Save and run your code.

Don't see anything? That's because it's displayed in the console. Open the console (as covered in the above instructions) and you should see "4"!

TYPE COERCION

In English, *coercion* means to force or persuade someone, typically by use of threats or punishment. *Type coercion* in JavaScript can be used when the operands of an operator are different data types (such as "string" and "number" – like: "five" + 5). Type coercion automatically converts one value to a compatible type to complete the operation. Let's try this out:

1. Update the code within your <body> element to this:

```
<body>
    <script>
    document.write("10" + 5);
    </script>
</body>
```

2. Save and run the code.

Good job! Many other programming languages would return an error if we were to include two different data types within an operation, but not JavaScript!

COMPARISON OPERATOR

In JavaScript, we can utilize double and triple equal signs to compare values.

== (double equal sign) is a symbol used to show that a comparison should be made. Specifically, this "==" symbol is an instruction to check whether the data on the left side of the symbol is equal to the data on the right side.

66

The answer to this comparison is an answer of "true" or "false."

When the "==" symbol is used to check for equality, usually it is used like this: [first item to be compared] == [second item to be compared]

For example: **(10 + 5) == 15**

In this example, we are asking the computer to check whether the result of adding 5 and 10 is equal to 15. The result would be "true."

Another example: **(10 + 6) == 15**

Here, the program would return "false," since (10 + 6) is not equal to 15.

Like all code, this is best understood by writing it out ourselves. Let's now return to using separate code files.

Complete these actions:

1. Open Test.html and edit the code within the <body> element as follows:

```
<body>
    <script src="Test_1.js">
    </script>
</body>
```

2. Open up Test_1.js and write this code:

```
document.write(10 == 10);
```

3. Run Test.html in the browser.

Great! This returns "true" because 10 is equal to 10.

To make the program return "false", simply change a number in your JavaScript code, such as:

```
document.write(5 == 10);
```

ANOTHER COMPARISON OPERATOR

=== (triple equal sign) is also used to show that a comparison should be made. Specifically, this "===" symbol is an instruction to check whether the data on the left side of the symbol is equal to the data on the right side, *and* that it is the same type of data (value type; data type) as that on the right. The answer to this comparison is always "true" or "false."

For example, let's say you want to check whether two birth dates are equal. You have two pieces of data in the computer that represent these two birth dates:

1) "DateOfBirth1" is data of type "Date", and the value of the data is "8/13/1985."

2) "DateOfBirth2" is data of type "Date", and the value of the data is "8/13/1985."

You would utilize the "===" symbol like this: **DateOfBirth1 === DateOfBirth2**

This tells the computer to check whether the two pieces of data are equal in both VALUE and TYPE. Since they are in this case, the program returns "true."

Now, if we changed the data type for DateOfBirth1 to a string, it would return false. Or if we changed the value of DateOfBirth2 to 3/27/83, it would return "false."

Let's see this in action by doing the following:

1. Write this JavaScript code within Test_1.js:

```
X = 10
Y = 10
document.write(X === Y);
```

2. Save it and run your HTML file.

Awesome! This returns "true" because they are both variables and both have the value 10.

You can change this to "false" by changing it to:

```
X = 10
Y = 5
document.write(X === Y);
```

Even though they are both variables, the values are different.

We can also return "false" by writing this JavaScript code:

```
X = "Ten"
document.write(X === 10);
```

LOGICAL OPERATORS

In JavaScript, there are three Boolean logical operators:

1) AND, which can be written as: **&&**

2) OR, which can be written as: **||**

3) NOT, which can be written as: **!**

The && operator performs the same function as AND covered earlier in this book, and verifies that two conditions are both true. If one or more is not true, it will return false.

For this step, let's include our JS code within our HTML code file.

Complete these actions:

1. Within an HTML file, write this code within the <body> element:

```
<body>
    <script>
    document.write(5 > 2 && 10 > 4);
    </script>
</body>
```

2. Save your file and run it.

Excellent job!

Our code returns "true" because five is greater than two, and ten is greater than four. We can make our code return "false" by changing one or both of the comparisons, such as:

```
<body>
    <script>
    document.write(5 > 10 && 10 > 4);
    </script>
</body>
```

The || (or) operator means the same as OR covered earlier. Let's put it into use by doing the following:

1. Write this code within the <body> element of your HTML file:

```
<body>
    <script>
    document.write(5 > 10 || 10 > 4);
    </script>
</body>
```

2. Save and execute your code.

Good work! It returned "true" because, while 5 is not greater than 10, 10 is greater than 4.

Or we can make it return "false" with the following code since neither is true:

```
<body>
    <script>
    document.write(5 > 10 || 10 > 20);
    </script>
</body>
```

The ! (not) operator checks whether or not something is true. If _____ is *not* present, "true" will be returned. For example: "If you are not 18, you cannot vote" would be something like: **if ! (age >= 18) then print "You cannot vote yet."**

To break this down, we are saying that if the user's age is NOT greater or equal to 18, the program should display "You cannot vote yet."

Let's put the ! operator into use by performing these actions:

1. Update the code within your <body> element as follows:

```
<body>
    <p id="Not"></p>
    <script>
    document.getElementById("Not").innerHTML = !(5 > 10);
    </script>
</body>
```

2. Save and run your code.

Good job! The result is "true" because *5* is *not* greater than 10.

And if you want a "double negative," write this code:

```
<body>
    <p id="Not"></p>
    <script>
    document.getElementById("Not").innerHTML = !!(20 > 10);
    </script>
```

Here we are saying that 20 is not not greater than 10.

TERNARY OPERATORS

Ternary means "made up of three parts." A *ternary operator* operates on three operands (a value or item used in a mathematical or logical operation): 1) a condition, 2) a value if the condition is true, and 3) a value if the condition is false.

Ternary operators can be used to assign a value to a variable, based on a condition. This is also referred to as a *conditional operator* because of the fact it assigns a value to a variable based on a condition.

The syntax for ternary operators (conditional operators) is: **Name_of_variable = (condition) ? Value_1:Value_2**

The ternary operator is a concise way to assign a value to a variable based on a condition.

We can make more sense of this by using it as follows:

1. Edit the code within the `<body>` element of your HTML file like this:

```
<body>
    <script>
    document.write(Bigger = (5 > 1) ? "The number on the left is bigger":
    "The number on the right is bigger");
    </script>
</body>
```

2. Save and execute your code.

Well done!

In this code, we said, "If it is true that 5 is bigger than 1, display 'The number on the left is bigger.'" If you change the numbers or flip the symbol to <, you can change the outcome of your code.

Input is a command that has the user input data. It allows users to type in information within your program.

With this data in mind, let's do something more elaborate with ternary operators by performing these actions:

1. Write this code within your `<body>` element in the HTML file:

```
<body>
    <p>Riders must be at least 52 centimeters tall to ride.</p>
    <input id="Height" value="52" />
    <button onclick="Ride_Function()">Click here</button>
    <p id="Ride"></p>
    <script>
    function Ride_Function() {
        var Height, Can_ride;
        Height = document.getElementById("Height").value;
        Can_ride = (Height < 52) ? "You are too short":"You are tall enough";
        document.getElementById("Ride").innerHTML = Can_ride + " to ride.";
    }
    </script>
</body>
```

2. Save and execute your code.

Good job! Go ahead and read through your code, line by line, to figure out what it does. Can you see which portion of the code includes the ternary operator?

NUMBER METHODS

Number methods assist you in working with numbers in JavaScript. There are several number methods. One of these is the toPrecision() method, which converts a number to a string with a set number of total digits, rounding it if necessary.

Complete these tasks:

1. Within the <body> element in your HTML file, write this code:

```
<body>
    <p id="Precision"></p>
    <script>
    var X = 12938.3012987376112;
    document.getElementById("Precision").innerHTML =
        X.toPrecision(10);
    </script>
</body>
```

2. Save and run your code.

Wonderful work! You should get "12938.30130" because we told the program to limit the output to 10 numbers and round it.

END OF CHAPTER CHALLENGE

Complete these actions:

1. Write a program that includes the following:

a. Boolean logic that returns "true,"

b. Type coercion, and

c. Display "false" in the console.log using Boolean logic.

2. Create a program that includes the following:

a. Double equal signs (==) and type coercion (i.e., use a variable and a value) and get a "true" result displayed, and

b. Triple equal signs (===) to produce "true" and "false."

3. Write a program that includes the following:

   a. A ternary operator, and

   b. The input command.

CHAPTER 8
OBJECT-ORIENTED PROGRAMMING BASICS

As we covered earlier, *objects* are items within computer programs that have both state and behavior. *Object-oriented* is an approach to programming that focuses on objects and data (as opposed to consecutive actions or some other approach).

You create objects by creating what are called *classes*. Classes are used to describe one or more objects. For example, we could create (or "declare") a class called a "Customer" class.

It is important to know that when you first create this class, you are describing the POTENTIAL characteristics and behavior of that TYPE of thing. You will still need to create an actual one of those things. That process is called "creating an INSTANCE" of the class, where "instance" means "an actual one" of the things described when you declared the class. When you do this, the data that makes up the object is kept in the computer's memory.

Instantiated refers to the process of creating a specific instance of an object from a class. Here is a diagram showing a car class with its instantiated objects:

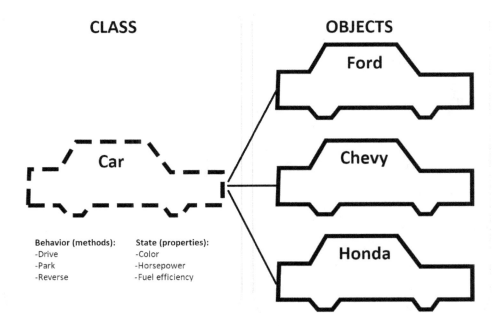

Let's look at another example. In a computer program designed to track pay records for all employees, you could have a class called "Employee".

Each program element representing an actual employee (Emily, Jack, Cherie, etc.) would be an instance of the "Employee" class. You would have one instance for each employee you entered into the computer.

Each time you created an "Employee" object, the computer would first find the "Employee" class, then use the definition of that class in creating that particular "Employee" instance using the data for the actual employee.

Consider this diagram, which shows a customer class, with its associated objects:

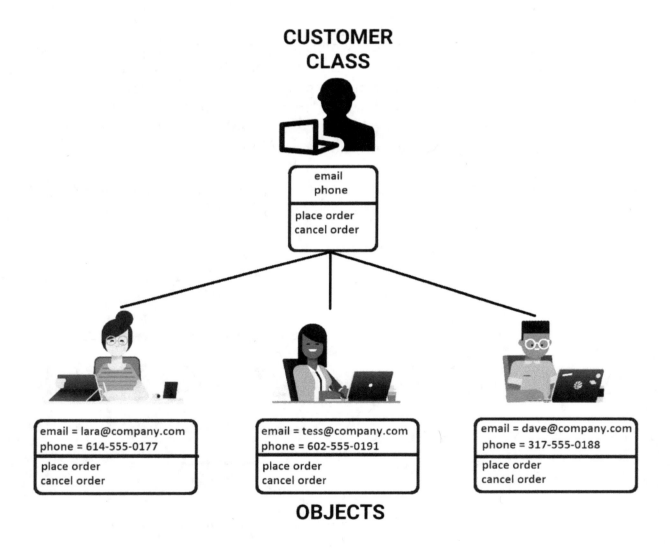

A *constructor* is a special part of a class (a template for defining an object). The constructor describes the default state of any new instance of the class that gets created. In other words, it gives default values for the properties of the class.

For example, let's look at a "Customer" class. The computer code to create the "Customer" class might look something like this:

```
class Customer
{
    string FullName;
    Boolean Active;
}
```

Now, let's say that whenever you created a new instance of the "Customer" class, you wanted it to be an active customer – in other words, you wanted the property "Active" to be set to "true".

To do this, you would make a constructor for the "Customer" class. It would be a small subprogram (function) inside the class that would be used every time an instance of the "Customer" class was created.

The constructor might look something like this:

```
Customer(string name) {
    FullName = name;
    Active = true;
}
```

The entire class would look like this:

```
class Customer
    {
    string FullName;
    Boolean Active;
    Customer(string name){
        Fullname = name;
        Active = true;
    }
}
```

The constructor would be used by asking for an instance of the "Customer" class to be created and passing along the desired name of the customer. The call (the act of execution) to create the instance of the class would look like this:

```
Customer cust = new Customer("Brenda Smith");
```

This creates a new instance of the "Customer" class using the constructor inside the class. The constructor uses the string "Brenda Smith" that it was given to set the value of the property "FullName" and uses the instruction in the constructor to set the property "Active" to "true."

The new instance of the "Customer" class, which is the variable "cust" here, will, therefore, have the properties:

```
FullName = "Brenda Smith";
Active = true;
```

(Note: The above code is given as an example and is not meant to be executed. We will create a constructor soon.)

KEYWORDS

As discussed earlier, JavaScript *keywords* identify actions to be performed. For example, var is a keyword we use to assign variables.

An important aspect to keywords is that they cannot be used to name variables or functions. For example: you can't say var var = "variable".

Another type of keyword is the "new" keyword, which is used to create new objects.

We also have the "this" keyword. The "this" keyword refers to the object that is currently executing the code. When used inside an object, "this" represents that object. When used within a function, "this" refers to the object that calls the function. For example, in a car object, if a function uses the "this" keyword to access the car's color, "this" will refer to the specific car object that owns the function, allowing the function to retrieve the car's color when called.

Now, we just covered a lot of information about constructors, the "new" keyword, the "this" keyword, and more. Let's put this all to use.

Perform these actions:

1. Open an HTML file, and within the `<body>` element write this code:

```html
<body>
    <p id="Keywords_and_Constructors"></p>
    <script>
    function Vehicle(Make, Model, Year, Color) {
        this.Vehicle_Make = Make;
        this.Vehicle_Model = Model;
        this.Vehicle_Year = Year;
        this.Vehicle_Color = Color;
    }
    var Jack = new Vehicle("Dodge", "Viper", 2021, "Red");
    var Emily = new Vehicle("Jeep", "Trail Hawk", 2020, "White and Black");
    var Erik = new Vehicle("Ford", "Pinto", 1971, "Mustard");
    document.getElementById("Keywords_and_Constructors").innerHTML =
    "Erik drives a " + Erik.Vehicle_Color + "-colored " + Erik.Vehicle_Model
    + " manufactured in " + Erik.Vehicle_Year;
    </script>
</body>
```

2. Save and execute your code.

Well done! This should print the following string: **Erik drives a Mustard-colored Pinto manufactured in 1971**

In this code, the function "Vehicle()" is an object constructor.

RESERVED WORDS

In JavaScript, there are certain words you cannot use as variables, labels (names assigned to sections of code), or functions. Examples of reserved words are: "true" and "false."

If you're interested, here is a URL to a list of the reserved words in JavaScript: www.w3schools.com/js/js_reserved.asp

The reason you cannot use these words is that they already mean something else – they are *reserved* for JavaScript.

IDENTIFIERS AND LITERALS

An *identifier* is a name for something. In JavaScript, identifiers are the names of variables, functions, keywords, and labels. In the following example code, "X" is the identifier: **var X = 10**

In contrast to an identifier, a *literal* is something that represents a value within *source code*. Source code is the version of a computer program as it was originally written by the developer of the program. It is called a literal because it directly represents the exact value to be used in the code, as opposed to an identifier, which only refers to or names a value.

Consider this code:

var X = 10

var Y = "Charlie"

The 10 is the integer (whole number) literal, Charlie is the string literal, and "X" and "Y" are the identifiers.

A literal is the data exactly as it is meant to be processed. Whereas an identifier is a name, the literal is the value itself.

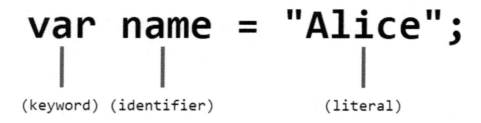

NESTED FUNCTIONS

Nested refers to something contained within something else. This can be a program within a program or a set of instructions inside another set of instructions.

A *subprogram* is any block of code that performs a specific task within a larger program. A function is a specific type of subprogram in JavaScript that can be called by name to execute its code and often returns a value, making it more focused on reuse and returning results compared to other types of subprograms. In other words, all functions are subprograms, but not all subprograms are functions. In JavaScript, a subprogram that is *not* a function could be a block of code that executes when a certain action occurs, such as a button click, without being assigned a specific name.

In coding, a *call* is a direction by a main computer program to execute the tasks of a subprogram (which, again, is a small program that is often used repeatedly to perform specific tasks).

More specifically, a call happens when a main program temporarily transfers control of the computer to a subprogram. Once the subprogram is done executing, control of the computer is returned to the main program. A program could make many "calls" to multiple subprograms as the program performs its sequence of tasks.

Here is a subprogram with a call written in pseudocode (normal English that looks similar to real code):

Subprogram GreetUser(name)
       Display "Hello, " + name + "!"
End Subprogram

Call GreetUser("Violet")

In this example, GreetUser is a subprogram that takes a name and displays a greeting message using that name. The *call* GreetUser("Violet") in the main program runs this subprogram with "Violet" as the value for name.

Sometimes a subprogram needs some information from the main program in order to perform its tasks. When the subprogram is created, its description might include this information. That information is called the *parameters* of the subprogram. Parameters are names used in a subprogram to represent the values that will be given to the function when it runs.

Here is a subprogram with parameters, written in pseudocode:

Subprogram CalculateSum(a, b)
      Sum = a + b
      Display "The sum is: " + Sum
End Subprogram

In this pseudocode, CalculateSum is a subprogram that takes two parameters (a and b), adds them together, and then displays the result.

Back to the concept of *nesting*. Again, nested refers to placing one structure (such as a function) inside another similar structure. The parameters of a nested section of code are described inside a bigger part that surrounds it.

It is called "nested" because it is placed inside something else. For example, a nested procedure is a smaller set of instructions contained within a larger procedure, allowing it to be run as part of the bigger sequence.

Here is this example written out in pseudocode:

```
Procedure CalculateArea()
        Input length, width
        Display "Calculating area..."

        Procedure MultiplyDimensions()
            Return length * width
        End Procedure

        area = MultiplyDimensions()

        Display "The area is: " + area
End Procedure

Call CalculateArea()
```

In this pseudocode, we define a procedure to calculate the area of a shape by taking the length and width as input, using the nested procedure (MultiplyDimensions) to multiply them, and then displaying the calculated area. As a note, there were no parameters in this example. Yet if we edit the last line of code to the following, the program would now have parameters (5, which represents the length, and 10, which is the width):

```
Call CalculateArea(5, 10)
```

The output of this example program would be:

Calculating area...
The area is: 50

In JavaScript, functions have access to the functions that are above them in the code. A nested function is a function under another function that is connected in some way.

We can make more sense of this all by completing these actions:

1. Within an HTML file, edit the code within the <body> element like this:

```
<body>
    <p id="Counting"></p>
    <script>
    document.getElementById("Counting").innerHTML = Count();
    function Count() {
        var Starting_point = 9;
        function Plus_one() {Starting_point += 1;}
        Plus_one();
        return Starting_point;
    }
    </script>
</body>
```

2. Save and execute your code.

Awesome work! "10" should be displayed. In our code, the Plus_one() function was the nested function.

SCOPE

In programming, code can have *scope*. Simply put, the scope is the functions, variables, and objects you have access to.

Scope can be limited or broad.

Variables have scope in that they can either be accessed by one, more than one, or all functions in a program.

The scope of variables is either *local* or *global*. In JavaScript, a global variable can be accessed from any function within the program, whereas a local variable is only accessed by the function it is assigned to.

Global variables are declared outside of functions, and local variables are declared inside of functions.

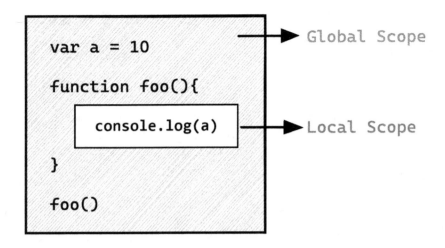

```
var a = 10

function foo(){

    console.log(a)

}

foo()
```

Global Scope

Local Scope

Complete these actions:

1. **Edit the code within the <body> element in an HTML file as follows:**

```
<body>
    <script>
    var X = 10;
    function Add_numbers_1() {
        document.write(20 + X + "<br>");
    }
    function Add_numbers_2() {
        document.write(X + 100);
    }
    Add_numbers_1();
    Add_numbers_2();
    </script>

</body>
```

(As a reminder, <br> is the break tag and creates a line break in text – like pressing enter on your keyboard.)

2. **Save and execute your code.**

Good job! It should return "30" and "110".

The variable X was assigned the value 10 outside of our function, but we still accessed it. Therefore, the above is an example of a global variable.

Now, let's try a local variable.

Perform these actions:

1. Write this code within the <body> element in your HTML file:

```
<body>
    <script>
    function Add_numbers_1() {
        var X = 10;
        document.write(20 + X + "<br>");
    }
    function Add_numbers_2() {
        document.write(X + 100);
        }
    Add_numbers_1();
    Add_numbers_2();
    </script>
</body>
```

2. Save and execute your code.

Good work!

This time, it only returns "30" because the variable was local – meaning, it was written within the function Add_numbers_1 and couldn't be accessed outside of it.

Let's say you wrote the above code and didn't understand why Add_numbers_2 didn't display a result. We could review the console using console.log() to help us debug our code. Perform these actions:

1. Change your code within the <body> element of the HTML code like this:

```
<body>
    <script>
    function Add_numbers_1() {
        var X = 10;
        console.log(15 + X);
    }
    function Add_numbers_2() {
        console.log(X + 100);
    }
    Add_numbers_1();
    Add_numbers_2();
    </script>
</body>
```

2. Save and execute your code.

You'll notice that no result is shown. Open the console, and there it is! It gives you the error "X is not defined." Knowing that data, we can debug our program!

AN OBJECT-ORIENTED PROGRAM

Now that you have the foundational knowledge in place, let's create a very basic object-oriented program.

Start with a new file and complete these actions:

1. Create a new HTML code file within Notepad++ and name it "oop.html". Within this new file, write this code:

```html
<!DOCTYPE html>
<head>
    <title>OOP Example</title>
</head>
<body>
    <h1>Check out the console</h1>
    <script src="oop.js"></script>
</body>
</html>
```

2. Save the file.

3. Create a new JavaScript code file within Notepad++ and name it "oop.js". Within this file, write this code:

```javascript
class Person {
    constructor(name, age) {
        this.name = name;
        this.age = age;
    }

    greet() {
        console.log(`Hello, my name is ${this.name} and I am ${this.age} years old.`);
    }
}

const person1 = new Person('Magnus', 25);
const person2 = new Person('Gideon', 30);
const person3 = new Person('Madeline', 35);


person1.greet();
person2.greet();
```

4. Save your JavaScript file.

5. Execute your HTML file (oop.html) in the browser. (Make sure to view the console to see the output.)

6. Now edit your JavaScript code to greet person3, and then re-execute your HTML in the browser.

Excellent work! In this program, you created a class and instantiated objects of that class.

END OF CHAPTER CHALLENGE

Complete these actions:

1. Write a program that includes the following:

   a. A class,

   b. A constructor,

   c. The "new" keyword, and

   d. The "this" keyword.

2. Perform the following actions:

   a. Write your own nested function,

   b. Assign a local variable, and

   c. Assign a global variable.

CHAPTER 9
CONDITIONAL STATEMENTS

As a reminder, a *conditional statement* is a programming element that allows the execution of certain blocks of code based on whether a specific condition or set of conditions evaluates to true or false, enabling decision-making within a program.

An *if statement* is a type of conditional statement that specifies that a section of code is to be executed *if* a condition is true.

Complete these actions:

1. Open an HTML file and edit the code within the <body> element as follows:

```
<body>
    <script>
    if (1 < 2) {
    document.write("The left number is smaller than the number on the right.")
    }
    </script>
</body>
```

2. Save and execute your code.

Well done! Since 1 is smaller than 2, the string is displayed.

The Date().getHours() method returns the hour in the specified date according to the local time, and the hours are listed as integers between 0 and 23. For example: 18 is equal to 6:00 p.m., 12 is noon, etc. It is similar to military time.

We can get creative with "if" statements. Do the following:

1. Within the <body> section of your code, write the following:

```
<body>
    <p id="Greeting">How are you this evening?</p>
    <script>
    if (new Date().getHours() < 18) {
        document.getElementById("Greeting").innerHTML = "How are you today?";
    }
    </script>
</body>
```

2. Save and execute your code.

Good job! In this program, we said, "If it is later than (greater than) 6:00 p.m. when I run my code, display 'How are you this evening?' If it is earlier than 6:00 p.m. when I run my code, 'How are you today?' will display."

So, what if we want more choices?

ELSE STATEMENTS

The *else statement* specifies a block of code that will be executed if the preceding condition(s) is false (opposite of the if statement). Let's put this into action.

Complete these actions:

1. Write this code within the `<body>` element of your HTML file:

```
<body>
    <p>Write your age:</p>
    <input id="Age" value="" />
    <p id="How_old_are_you?"></p>
    <button onclick="Age_Function()">Click here</button>
    <script>
    function Age_Function() {
        Age = document.getElementById("Age").value;
        if (Age >= 18) {
            Vote = "You are old enough to vote!";
        }
        else {
            Vote = "You are not old enough to vote!";
        }
        document.getElementById("How_old_are_you?").innerHTML = Vote;
        }
    </script>
</body>
```

2. Save and execute your code.

Good job! You just created a program that determines if a person can vote.

Now, what if we want even more choices?

ELSE IF

The "else if" statement follows an "if" statement and is executed in the case the "if" statement is found to be false.

For example: 1) If hungry, eat. 2) Else if thirsty, drink. 3) Else, rest.

Perform these actions:

1. Edit the code within your <body> element as follows:

```
<body>
    <p id="Time_of_day"></p>
    <script>
    function Time_function() {
        var Time = new Date().getHours();
        var Reply;
        if (Time < 12 == Time > 0) {
            Reply = "It is morning time!";
        }
        else if (Time > 12 == Time < 18) {
            Reply = "It is the afternoon.";
        }
        else {
            Reply = "It is evening time.";
        }
        document.getElementById("Time_of_day").innerHTML = Reply;
    }
    Time_function();
    </script>
</body>
```

2. Save and run your code.

Wonderful! You made a program that pulls the time from your computer and tells you what time of day it is using conditional statements.

LET AND CONST

As you know, a *keyword* in programming is a reserved word (a word in programming that cannot be used as a variable or function name because it has a predefined function in the language) that has a specific meaning and purpose in the language's syntax. For example, *var* and *if* are keywords in JavaScript.

let is a keyword used for variables that may change, but are only needed within a specific block of code.

const (short for *constant*) is a keyword used for variables that should not change after their initial value is set.

92

A programmer might use const to store a constant value that should not change, like the number of hours in a day. On the other hand, they may use let for a variable that might change later, such as tracking the current hour of the day.

Let's put these two keywords into use by building a simple program that runs until the user's score reaches 100, by performing these actions:

1. Create a new HTML code file within Notepad++ and name it "score.html". Within this file, write this code and then save it:

```html
<!DOCTYPE html>
<head>
    <title>Score Program</title>
</head>
<body>
    <h1>Check the console for score updates!</h1>
    <script src="score.js"></script>
</body>
</html>
```

2. Create a new JavaScript code file within Notepad++ and name it "score.js". Within this file, write this code:

```javascript
const maxScore = 100;
let currentScore = 0;
```

This sets the maximum score to 100 (which cannot change), and the initial score to 0 (which can change).

3. Next, below the code from the previous step, write this function:

```javascript
function increaseScore() {
    if (currentScore < maxScore) {
        currentScore += 10;
        console.log(`Current Score: ${currentScore}`);

    if (currentScore >= maxScore) {
        console.log('You reached the maximum score!');
        clearInterval(scoreInterval);
        }
    }
}
```

This function checks if the current score is less than the maximum, adds 10 to the score, displays the new score, and stops the score increase once the maximum score is reached.

4. Finally, below your function, write this:

```
let scoreInterval = setInterval(increaseScore, 1000);
```

This line repeatedly calls the increaseScore() function every 1000 milliseconds (which is one second), storing the interval ID in the scoreInterval variable so it can later be stopped using clearInterval().

Here is what your full JavaScript code should look like:

```
const maxScore = 100;
let currentScore = 0;

function increaseScore() {
        if (currentScore < maxScore) {
                currentScore += 10;
                console.log(`Current Score: ${currentScore}`);

        if (currentScore >= maxScore) {
                console.log('You reached the maximum score!');
                clearInterval(scoreInterval);
                }
        }
}

let scoreInterval = setInterval(increaseScore, 1000);
```

This program automatically increases the score by 10 every second and displays the updated score in the console until it reaches the maximum score of 100. It uses setInterval() to repeatedly call the increaseScore() function, which increments the score and stops once the maximum is reached using clearInterval().

5. Save your code.

6. Run the score.html file.

You will need to open the console in order to view the score increasing. So, ensure to open it and then refresh the page so you can watch the program execute.

Well done! You created a basic program that included the let and const keywords!

SWITCH STATEMENT

A *control structure* is a programming tool that determines the order in which code executes based on specific conditions or logic.

A real-world example of a control structure would be a traffic light: if the light is green, cars go; if it's yellow, they slow down; and if it's red, they stop. The decision (go, slow, stop) depends on the current color of the light, just like how a control structure in programming directs the flow based on conditions.

A control statement is a broad term that embraces conditional statements, and other structures that control the flow of a program.

As a reminder, an *expression* is a value or variable that is being tested in a statement, such as a number, a string, or the result of a calculation.

The *switch statement* is a control structure that checks a value or expression and runs specific blocks of code depending on which value it matches, which can be useful when you have multiple possible outcomes for a variable.

Let's say you have a situation where you need to decide what action to take based on the current day of the week. In a switch statement, the day of the week acts as the condition, and for each possible day (like Monday, Tuesday, etc.), there is a specific action to take (such as acknowledging the start of the workweek or midweek). If the day does not match any of the predefined days, a default action is taken (like concluding it is an invalid day). This structure allows for clean, organized decision-making based on multiple possible outcomes. All of this will make more sense when we write out the upcoming code.

A *case* in a switch statement represents one possible value that the variable or condition being checked could have. When the variable's value matches a specific case, the code associated with that case is executed. In the "days of the week" example, each day is a case.

default is an optional section in the switch statement that runs if none of the case values match the expression. It acts like a fallback option. To take up our "days of the week" example again, if the case is an unknown day of the week, the default action could be a response like "Invalid day".

break is a command that stops the code from running the next case once a match is found. Without break, the code would continue running the following cases even if a match has already been found. In the "days of the week" example, if the break command is used after "Tuesday", the code stops once it prints "Second day of the week". Without break, it would continue running and print the actions for "Wednesday", "Thursday", and "Friday", even though Tuesday was already matched.

Here is another example of the switch statement written in pseudocode:

variable color = "Red"

switch (color)

> **case "Red":**
> > **Display "Stop"**
> > **break**
>
> **case "Yellow":**
> > **Display "Caution"**
> > **break**
>
> **case "Green":**
> > **Display "Go"**
> > **break**
>
> **default:**
> > **Display "Unknown color"**

end switch

This example program uses a switch statement to check the value of the color variable and displays "Stop" if the color is "Red", "Caution" if it's "Yellow", "Go" if it's "Green", and "Unknown color" if the color does not match any of the predefined cases. Since the variable is assigned the value "Red", the program will return "Stop".

Now that we have defined these terms, let's write an actual program that puts this data into use.

Complete these actions:

1. Create a new HTML code file within Notepad++ and name it "switch.html". Within this file, write this code and then save it:

```html
<!DOCTYPE html>
<head>
    <title>My Switch Statement</title>
    <script src="switch.js" defer></script>
</head>
<body>
    <h1>The Day of the Week</h1>

    <label for="daySelect">Select a day:</label>
    <select id="daySelect">
        <option value="Monday">Monday</option>
        <option value="Tuesday">Tuesday</option>
        <option value="Wednesday">Wednesday</option>
        <option value="Thursday">Thursday</option>
        <option value="Friday">Friday</option>
        <option value="Saturday">Saturday</option>
        <option value="Sunday">Sunday</option>
    </select>

    <button onclick="getDayAction()">Get Action</button>

    <p id="result"></p>
</body>
</html>
```

This code creates a webpage where users can pick a day from a dropdown menu and see a related message. The *defer attribute* in the <script> tag makes sure that the JavaScript file is loaded and executed only after the HTML content has fully loaded, preventing any issues with accessing elements before they exist. <label> is a text description for the dropdown, and its *for attribute* connects it to the dropdown, so clicking the label will highlight the menu. The <select> element creates the dropdown, and each option inside it (<option>) is a different day. The value of each option is the specific data used by the program when the user picks that day from the dropdown. This will make more sense once we execute it in conjunction with our JavaScript Code.

2. Create a new JavaScript code file within Notepad++ and name it "switch.js".

97

Within switch.js, write this code:

```javascript
function getDayAction() {
    let day = document.getElementById("daySelect").value;
    let result = '';

    switch (day) {
        case 'Monday':
            result = 'Start of the workweek. Let\'s be productive!';
            break;
        case 'Tuesday':
            result = 'Second day of the week. Keep the momentum!';
            break;
        case 'Wednesday':
            result = 'Midweek already. You\'re halfway there!';
            break;
        case 'Thursday':
            result = 'Almost the weekend. Stay focused!';
            break;
        case 'Friday':
            result = 'It\'s Friday! Finish strong!';
            break;
        case 'Saturday':
            result = 'It\'s the weekend! Time to relax!';
            break;
        case 'Sunday':
            result = 'Rest day. Recharge for the week ahead!';
            break;
        default:
            result = 'Invalid day selected.';
    }

    document.getElementById("result").textContent = result;
}
```

3. Save your code.

4. Execute switch.html in the browser, select a day of the week using the dropdown, click "Get Action", and then view the output.

Good job! You successfully utilized a switch statement. This is the fourth conditional statement available for use in JavaScript (with *if, else if,* and *else,* being the other three).

STRING METHODS

JavaScript has *string methods* that allow you to perform tasks with strings.

As covered earlier, programming languages have certain data types built into them. These built-in data types are the most basic data types in the programming language and are referred to as *primitive* data types. One of the key traits of a primitive data type is that it cannot be simplified any further. A primitive data type is a predefined type of data that is built into the language.

There are seven primitive data types in JavaScript – these are:

1. **Number:** Represents both integers and floating-point numbers, such as 182 or 3.14.

2. **String:** Represents textual data, like "The Tech Academy".

3. **Boolean:** Represents a logical value (either true or false).

4. **Undefined:** Indicates a variable that has been declared but not assigned a value, such as:

   var myVariable;

5. **Null:** Represents a deliberate assignment of no value to a variable, indicating the variable is intentionally set to have no object or data, such as:

   var myVariable = null;

6. **Symbol:** Represents a unique identifier, useful in more complex scenarios. Here's an example of using a Symbol in JavaScript:

   const uniqueId = Symbol('id');
   console.log(uniqueId);

   In this example, Symbol('id') creates a unique identifier with the description "id" and the output would be Symbol(id). Even if you create another symbol with the same description, it will still be unique:

   const anotherId = Symbol('id');
   console.log(uniqueId === anotherId);

   This output would be: false. Each symbol, even with the same description, is guaranteed to be unique, making it useful in certain, uncommon scenarios.

7. **BigInt:** Allows representation of integers larger than the Number type can handle.

Everything else (non-primitive data types) are objects. Objects are created by the programmer, not predefined and built into the programming language.

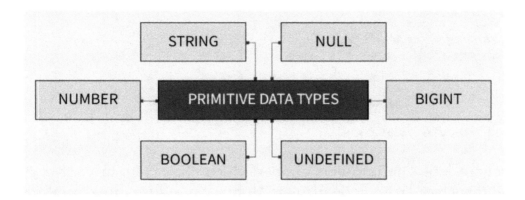

Back to string methods, the concat() method is a string method that concatenates (connects) two or more strings. So let's use it!

Complete these actions:

1. Write this code within the \<body\> section of an HTML file:

```
<body>
    <p id="Concatenate"></p>
    <script>
    var part_1 = "I have ";
    var part_2 = "made this ";
    var part_3 = "into a complete ";
    var part_4 = "sentence.";
    var whole_sentence = part_1.concat(part_2, part_3, part_4);
    document.getElementById("Concatenate").innerHTML = whole_sentence;
    </script>
</body>
```

2. Save and execute your code.

Great work! It displays the sentence as a whole.

SLICE() METHOD

The slice() method is a string method that extracts a section of a string and then returns the extracted section in a new string.

Complete these actions:

1. Write this code within the `<body>` element of an HTML file:

```
<body>
    <p id="Slice"></p>
    <script>
    var Sentence = "All work and no play makes Johnny a dull boy.";
    var Section = Sentence.slice(27,33);
    document.getElementById("Slice").innerHTML = Section;
    </script>
</body>
```

2. Save and execute your code.

Excellent job! The numbers choose which characters in your string will be cut out and displayed. Your code displays "Johnny" because those are the characters that are located between 27-33.

Here are two points to keep in mind:

1) Computers start counting at 0 – not 1.

2) The spaces are included in the count.

END OF CHAPTER CHALLENGE

Complete these actions:

1. Write your own function that contains an "if" statement, "else if" statement and "else" statement.

2. Edit score.js and successfully execute score.html as follows:

• Change the speed of the score increase (more or less than the current 1000 milliseconds).

• Increase the score by a different amount (more or less than 10 "points" at a time).

3. Edit switch.js as follows:

• Write a switch statement that prints a greeting based on the current time of day (morning, afternoon, or evening).

CHAPTER 10
LOOPS

In normal English, a *loop* is something that connects back to the beginning point.

In programming, a loop is a sequence of instructions that are continually repeated until an exact condition is achieved. Usually it would be where a certain set of actions are performed by a computer program, then the program checks to see if it has reached the condition required for completion. If not, it starts over and repeats the set of actions. If so, it exits the loop and moves on to the next consecutive instruction in the computer program.

For example, you could direct the computer to search through a list of paint colors until the color "red" is found. The list the computer will search is this:
- Blue
- Yellow
- Red
- Orange
- White

Here is what it could look like in pseudocode:

Step 1: Get the next consecutive item in the list.

Step 2: Check whether the item equals "Red."

Step 3: If the item equals "Red," exit this loop.

Step 4: If the item is not equal to "Red," loop back to step 1.

When this loop is executed, it will run like this:

Step 1: Acquired "Blue."

Step 2: Checked if item "Blue" is equal to "Red"

Step 3: Item not equal to "Red." Did not exit the loop.

Step 4: Item not equal to "Red." Looped back to Step 1.

Step 1: Acquired "Yellow."

Step 2: Checked if item "Yellow" is equal to "Red."

Step 3: Item not equal to "Red." Did not exit the loop.

Step 4: Item not equal to "Red." Looped back to Step 1.

Step 1: Acquired "Red."

Step 2: Checked if item "Red" is equal to "Red."

Step 3: Item equal to "Red." Exited the loop.

In normal English, *iterate* means to do something repeatedly.

In coding, iterate has a similar meaning: to say or do something again; to repeat an action.

An *iteration* is the act of repeating. It means to go through a defined series of actions, repeating a certain number of times. Usually this defined series of actions is repeated a certain number of times, or until a condition is met.

Computer programs are usually created in iterations: Coming up with a basic working version, reviewing the program for mistakes to correct and improvements to make, doing that work, and repeating. When the program works acceptably, this process ends.

In JavaScript, the "while loop" means that "while (blank) is occurring, do (blank)."

A while loop is basically a repeating "if statement." Meaning, you are telling the computer to execute certain code repeatedly while a particular condition is present.

For example: While hungry, eat.

A while loop loops through a block of code for as long as a specified condition is true.

Here is a while loop diagrammed:

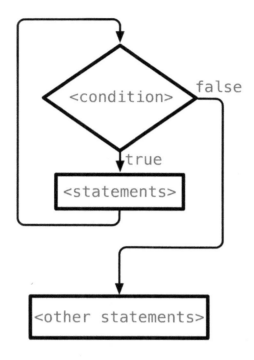

Let's create a while loop in JavaScript by completing these actions:

1. **Create a new JavaScript code file and name it "loop.js." Within this JS file, write this code:**

```javascript
function count_To_Ten() {
    var Digit = "";
    var X = 1;
    while (X < 11) {
      Digit += "<br>" + X;
      X++;
    }
    document.getElementById("Counting_to_Ten").innerHTML = Digit;
}
```

   This is a function that includes a while loop inside of it. We use the `<br>` tag within our string to cause spacing between lines of text. ++ is used to increment (add one) in JavaScript. To decrement (subtract one) we use - -. In this block of code, we are telling the program to run while X is less than 11 - meaning, it will stop once it reaches 10.

2. **Save your code.**

3. **Create a new HTML code file and name it "loop.html."**

4. Within loop.html, write this code:

```html
<!DOCTYPE html>
<head>
    <title>Loop</title>
</head>
<body>
    <p id="Counting_to_Ten"></p>
    <button onclick="count_To_Ten()">Click here to start.</button>
    <script src="loop.js"></script>
</body>
</html>
```

5. Save and execute loop.html in the browser.

Well done! The output of this code is 1-10.

ARRAYS

An *array* is a collection of data arranged in rows and columns. It is a group of related things that are stored together in a sequence.

In coding, arrays are used to organize items in a logical way. They can be quite simple, or quite complex.

A simple array would be something like the numbers 7, 3, and 15. It could be written out like this: **[7, 3, 15]**

These three pieces of data are called *elements* – they are the elements of the array. Another word for the data in an element is *value*. The first element in the array here has a value of "7".

A system is needed for identifying each element of an array. The simplest method for this is to start numbering them at zero starting at the left position and count up from there. In the above example, the element "7" would be at position 0, "3" would be at position 1 and "15" would be at position 2.

Another word for the position of an element is the *index* of the element – for the above example of an array, index 0 is "7", index 1 is "3", etc.

Each element, therefore, has two properties: its index and its value.

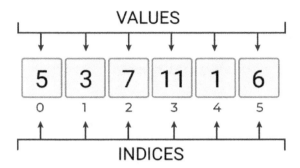

(The plural of *index* is *indices* or *indexes*.)

Let's say you have three pictures of your cat and you could save them in an array: "CatPic1", "CatPic2", and "CatPic3".

The array would look like this: **["CatPic1,""CatPic2,""CatPic3"]**

Here, the element at index 1 has a value of "CatPic2".

Arrays are objects and, so, are included in the object data type. As you know, objects can have properties (characteristics) and methods (actions). Arrays are a special type of object.

Let's create an array by completing these actions:

1. Open your loop.js file and write this code:

```
function cat_pics(){
    var Cat_Picture = [];
    Cat_Picture[0] = "sleeping";
    Cat_Picture[1] = "playing";
    Cat_Picture[2] = "eating";
    Cat_Picture[3] = "purring";
    document.getElementById("Cat").innerHTML = "In this picture, the cat is " +
        Cat_Picture[2] + ".";
}
```

In this code, we created an array of "cat pictures" in JavaScript.

2. Save your code.

3. Open your HTML file (loop.html) and, within the <body> element, write:

```
<p id="Cat"></p>
<button onclick="cat_pics()">Click here.</button>
```

Please note: you can delete the HTML code that you wrote in the preceding assignment.

4. Save and execute loop.html in the browser.

Excellent work! This would display the sentence: **In this picture, the cat is eating.**

In the above array, "Cat_Picture" is the object. 0, 1, 2 and 3 are the indices and "sleeping," "playing," "eating" and "purring" are the properties of the object.

FOR LOOPS

A "for loop" is used to repeat a section of code a number of times.

For loops are used when the number of iterations is known.

For example: **for each student in the class (25), provide a grade.**

The for loop repeatedly executes instructions as long as a particular condition is true.

You can see a diagram of a for loop on the following page.

Here is a for loop:

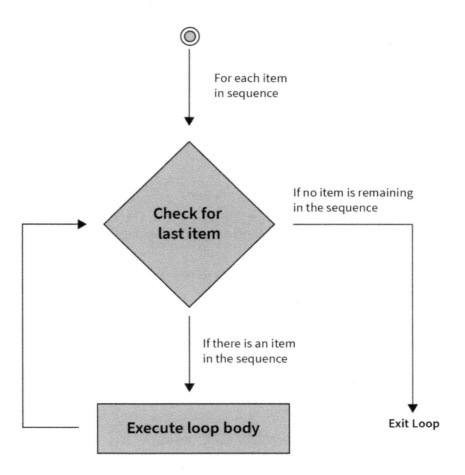

Complete these actions:

1. Open your loop.js file and write this code:

```
var Instruments = ["Guitar", "Drums", "Piano", "Bass", "Violin", "Trumpet", "Flute"];
var Content = "";
var Y;
function for_Loop() {
    for (Y = 0; Y < Instruments.length; Y++) {
    Content += Instruments[Y] + "<br>";
    }
    document.getElementById("List_of_Instruments").innerHTML = Content;
}
```

var Content declares an empty string variable Content to store the instrument list as it's being built. The for loop iterates through the Instruments array, adding each instrument name to the Content string with a line break (<br>), and then updates an HTML element with the ID List_of_Instruments to display the resulting list.

2. Save your code.

3. Open your HTML file (loop.html) and, within the <body> element, write:

```
<p id="List_of_Instruments"></p>
<button onclick="for_Loop()">Click here.</button>
```

   Please note: you can delete the HTML code that you wrote in the preceding assignment.

4. Save and execute loop.html in the browser.

   Good work! The output of this code should be the list of instruments.

   Writing a loop was useful here because we didn't have to individually write a document.write() method for each instrument.

DO...WHILE LOOP

   A "do...while loop" is similar to a while loop, but it ensures that the block of code runs at least once before checking the condition.

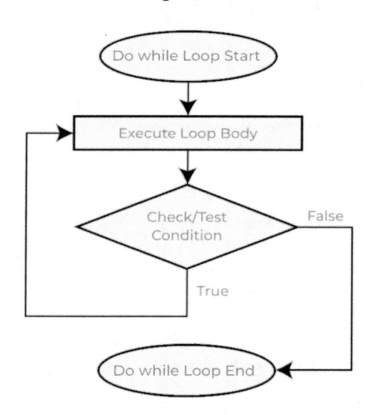

Let's create a do...while loop as follows:

1. Open your loop.js file and write this code:

```javascript
const rollDiceBtn = document.getElementById('rollDiceBtn');
const result = document.getElementById('result');

rollDiceBtn.addEventListener('click', function() {
    let dice;
    let rolls = '';

    do {
        dice = Math.floor(Math.random() * 6) + 1;
        rolls += `Rolled: ${dice}<br>`;
    } while (dice !== 6);

    result.innerHTML = rolls + "You rolled a 6!";
});
```

(This code selects a button and a paragraph element from the HTML file, and when the button is clicked, it rolls a dice repeatedly until a 6 is rolled, displaying each roll in the paragraph and adding a final message when the 6 is rolled.)

2. Save your code.

3. Open loop.html and, within the <body> element, write:

```html
<h1>Roll the Dice</h1>
<button id="rollDiceBtn">Roll Dice</button>
<p id="result"></p>
<script src="loop.js"></script> </body>
```

Please note: you can delete the HTML code that you wrote in the preceding assignment.

4. Save and execute loop.html in the browser.

END OF CHAPTER CHALLENGE

Complete these actions:

1. Write a while loop that keeps doubling a number until it exceeds 1000.

2. Create an array with the names of five countries you would like to visit, and print each value to the console.

3. Write a for loop that counts backwards from 100 to 0 in steps of 5 and displays each number.

4. (This step will require online research and covers some skills we have not taught you.) Write a program that:

    a. Utilizes the toUpperCase() method, and

    b. Utilizes the search() method.

CHAPTER 11
FINAL ASSIGNMENTS

Now that you have learned the basics of HTML and JavaScript, let's put it all together by creating a timer that will countdown by seconds!

Complete these actions:

1. Create a new HTML file and write this code:

```
<!DOCTYPE html>
<html>
    <body>
        <p>How many seconds would you like to set your alarm for?</p>
        <input id="seconds" value="" />
        <button onclick="countdown()">Click here</button>
        <p id="timer"></p>
        <script>
        function countdown() {
            var seconds = document.getElementById("seconds").value;

            function tick() {
                seconds = seconds - 1;
                timer.innerHTML = seconds;
                var time = setTimeout(tick, 1000);
            if (seconds == -1) {
                alert("Time's up!");
                clearTimeout(time);
                timer.innerHTML = "";
            }
            }
            tick();
        }
        </script>
    </body>
</html>
```

The code included above has been explained earlier in this book, but if there is anything you do not understand, ensure to define it through online research.

2. Save and execute your code in the browser.

3. Through online research, figure out how to end the program (i.e, stop the countdown) when a user clicks the OK button on the alert box.

Good job on creating this countdown program!

SNAKE GAME

Remember the popular computer game "Snake" – where you move a snake around and eat apples, growing with each bite? Let's build it with HTML, CSS and JavaScript!

Complete these actions:

1. Write, save and execute this code (it's a lot!):

```html
<!DOCTYPE html>
<html>
<head>
    <title>Snake Game</title>
    <style>
        /* Style section: Centers the game canvas and sets its border and background */
        body {
            display: flex;
            justify-content: center;
            align-items: center;
            height: 95vh;
        }
        #gameCanvas {
            border: 1px solid darkblue;
            background-color: #F0F0F0;
        }
    </style>
</head>
<body>
    <!-- Game board/canvas where the snake game will be displayed -->
    <canvas id="gameCanvas" width="600" height="600"></canvas>
    <script>
        // Getting the canvas element and setting up for drawing
        const canvas = document.getElementById('gameCanvas');
        const ctx = canvas.getContext('2d');

        // Setting up game variables such as scale, rows, and columns
        const scale = 10;
        const rows = canvas.height / scale;
        const columns = canvas.width / scale;
        let snake;

        // Game start function
        (function setup() {
            snake = new Snake();
            fruit = new Fruit();
            fruit.pickLocation();

            // Game loop - updates and draws the snake and fruit regularly
            window.setInterval(() => {
                ctx.clearRect(0, 0, canvas.width, canvas.height);
                fruit.draw();
                snake.update();
                snake.draw();
```

(continued on the next page...)

113

```javascript
        // Checks if the snake has eaten the fruit
        if (snake.eat(fruit)) {
            fruit.pickLocation();
        }

        // Checks for collision with the snake's tail
        snake.checkCollision();
    }, 125);
}());
// Keyboard control for snake's movement
window.addEventListener('keydown', e => {
    const direction = e.key.replace('Arrow', '');
    snake.changeDirection(direction);
});

// Snake creation function
function Snake() {
    this.x = 0;
    this.y = 0;
    this.xSpeed = scale * 1;
    this.ySpeed = 0;
    this.total = 0;
    this.tail = [];

    // Function to draw the snake on the canvas
    this.draw = function() {
        ctx.fillStyle = "green";
        for (let i = 0; i < this.tail.length; i++) {
            ctx.fillRect(this.tail[i].x, this.tail[i].y, scale, scale);
        }
        ctx.fillRect(this.x, this.y, scale, scale);
    };

    // Function to update the snake's position
    this.update = function() {
        for (let i = 0; i < this.tail.length - 1; i++) {
            this.tail[i] = this.tail[i + 1];
        }
        this.tail[this.total - 1] = { x: this.x, y: this.y };

        this.x += this.xSpeed;
        this.y += this.ySpeed;

        // Wrap around logic for the snake to appear on the opposite side
        if (this.x >= canvas.width) {
            this.x = 0;
        }

        if (this.y >= canvas.height) {
            this.y = 0;
        }

        if (this.x < 0) {
            this.x = canvas.width;
        }

        if (this.y < 0) {
            this.y = canvas.height;
        }
    };
```

(continued on the next page...)

114

```javascript
        // Function to change the direction of the snake
        this.changeDirection = function(direction) {
            switch(direction) {
                case 'Up':
                    this.xSpeed = 0;
                    this.ySpeed = -scale * 1;
                    break;
                case 'Down':
                    this.xSpeed = 0;
                    this.ySpeed = scale * 1;
                    break;
                case 'Left':
                    this.xSpeed = -scale * 1;
                    this.ySpeed = 0;
                    break;
                case 'Right':
                    this.xSpeed = scale * 1;
                    this.ySpeed = 0;
                    break;
            }
        };

        // Function to check if the snake has eaten the fruit
        this.eat = function(fruit) {
            if (this.x === fruit.x && this.y === fruit.y) {
                this.total++;
                return true;
            }

            return false;
        };

        // Function to check if the snake has collided with its tail
        this.checkCollision = function() {
            for (var i = 0; i < this.tail.length; i++) {
                if (this.x === this.tail[i].x && this.y === this.tail[i].y) {
                    this.total = 0;
                    this.tail = [];
                }
            }
        };
}
// Fruit setup function
function Fruit() {
    this.x;
    this.y;

    // Function to randomly place the fruit on the canvas
    this.pickLocation = function() {
        this.x = (Math.floor(Math.random() * columns - 1) + 1) * scale;
        this.y = (Math.floor(Math.random() * rows - 1) + 1) * scale;
    };
```

(continued on the next page...)

```
            // Function to draw the fruit on the canvas
         this.draw = function() {
            ctx.fillStyle = "red";
            ctx.fillRect(this.x, this.y, scale, scale);
         };
      }
   </script>
</body>
</html>
```

Please note that there is some CSS code here (within the <style> element). This is an excellent self-teaching opportunity for you, which again is a vital programming skill. Ensure to define any code in this program that you do not understand (including CSS) through online research.

By the way, in case this is helpful, here is a link to the full code for this game: bit.ly/techacademyfulljs

2. Save and run your code in the browser. (Please note: after you write and run the code, you will need to click on the game board before being able to move the snake with the arrow keys.)

3. Through online research, make these edits to your program:

a. Change the color of the snake and fruit.

b. Alter the speed of the snake.

Well done on creating a basic video game with HTML, CSS, and JavaScript!

CONGRATULATIONS!

You have reached the end of our book! Well done for your hard work and persistence!

You should now have a basic understanding of JavaScript and coding. We have successfully laid a firm foundation on which to build upon. Now that you have these basics in place, you can excel your skills to build more advanced websites and software.

To accomplish taking your skill set to the next level, read the next book in this series! In it, we will teach you new tools and how to build stronger programs.

Thank you for your time and attention, and good luck!

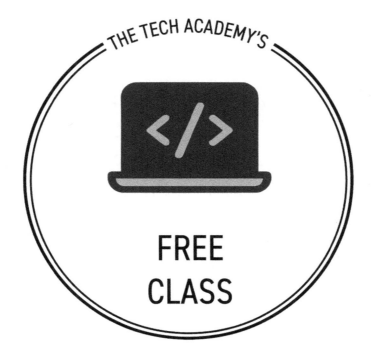

OTHER READING

Be sure to check out other Tech Academy books, which are all available for purchase on Amazon:

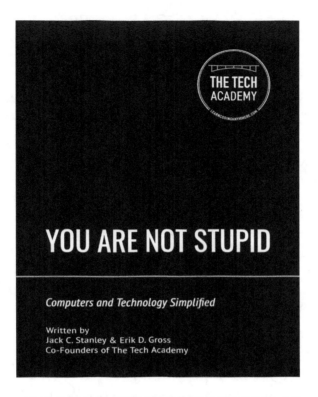

Learn Coding Basics in Hours with Small Basic

Programming for Absolute Beginners

Written by: Jack C. Stanley & Erik D. Gross,
Co-Founders of The Tech Academy

Learn Coding Basics in Hours with Python

Programming for Absolute Beginners

Written by: Jack C. Stanley & Erik D. Gross,
Co-Founders of The Tech Academy

PROJECT MANAGEMENT HANDBOOK

Simplified Agile, Scrum and DevOps for Beginners

Written by
Jack C. Stanley & Erik D. Gross
Co-Founders of The Tech Academy